Mason Gallagher

A Chapter of Unwritten History

The Protestant Episcopacy of the revolutionary patriots. Lost and restored.

Mason Gallagher

A Chapter of Unwritten History

The Protestant Episcopacy of the revolutionary patriots. Lost and restored.

ISBN/EAN: 9783337308810

Printed in Europe, USA, Canada, Australia, Japan

Cover: Foto ©ninafisch / pixelio.de

More available books at **www.hansebooks.com**

𝔄 Chapter of Unwritten History.

THE PROTESTANT EPISCOPACY

OF THE

REVOLUTIONARY PATRIOTS.

LOST AND RESTORED.

A Centennial Offering,

BY

Rev. MASON GALLAGHER,

Author of True Churchmanship Vindicated: The Primitive Eirenicon: Revision a Duty and Necessity.

"I Have Somewhat Against Thee Because Thou Hast Left Thy First Love. Remember Therefore From Whence Thou art Fallen, And Repent, And Do The First Works. . . . What The Spirit Saith Unto The Churches." REVELATION, II. 4, 5, 7.

PHILADELPHIA:
REFORMED EPISCOPAL ROOMS,
931 ARCH STREET,
1883.

PREFACE.

The present work, to which the notes are attached, is a portion of an address delivered on the Ninth Anniversary of the Organization of the Reformed Episcopal Church, to the R. E. congregation, of Boston, on December 3d, 1882.

After a membership of over thirty years in the Protestant Episcopal Church, and over ten years instruction in its seminaries, the author was ignorant of some of the important facts presented in this treatise. If his instructors were cognizant of them they kept the knowledge to themselves. Since his connection with the Reformed Episcopal Church he has been privileged to become acquainted with transactions of such great interest and importance. Of greater interest, inasmuch as the organization of the Reformed Episcopal Church is thereby more fully vindicated. Interesting facts connected with the subject have been omitted for want of space.

There is one point of peculiar interest not dwelt upon in the notes, which we are unwilling entirely to pass over. The position and action of John Jay, the illustrious Chief Justice of our Nation, has been described; we rejoice to know that Washington held similar views, and was a truly Reformed Episcopalian, in full accord with Mr. Jay. The spirit of Christian charity and unity in both was pre-eminent. All may contemplate and imitate them with profit.

We read that "Mr. Jay finding, on his removal to Bedford, no Episcopal church in the vicinity, constantly attended one belonging to the Presbyterians: nor did he scruple to unite with his fellow Christians of that persuasion in commemorating the passion of their common Lord." Life I, 434.

When Washington was encamped with his army at Morristown, he sent a note to Rev. Dr. Johns, the Presbyterian pastor, inquiring whether he would be welcome to partake of the semi-annual Communion in his church on the following Lord's day. He stated that he was a member of the Church of England, but was without exclusive partialities as a Christian. He accepted a cordial invitation, and received with his fellow Christians of other names, the memorial of the dying love of their common Lord. Sparks' Washington, p. 524. Appendix to McGuire's Religious Opinions of Washington.

The difference in sentiment on this important topic is also manifest in his reply to the address of the General Convention of the Protestant Episcopal Church, August 1789. "On this occasion," he writes, "it would ill become me to conceal the joy I have felt in perceiving the fraternal affection, which appears to increase every day among the friends of genuine religion. It affords edifying prospects indeed, to see Christians of different denominations, dwell together in more charity and conduct themselves with respect to each other, with a more Christian-like spirit than ever they have done in any former age, or in any other nation. GEORGE WASHINGTON."

When one considers the offensiveness of language and action which unfortunately so largely characterizes the Protestant Episcopal Church, with respect to fellowship with the greater bodies of Evangelical Christians around them, it is refreshing to contemplate the spirit and action of these two greatest and grandest of American Episcopal laymen. Reformed Episcopalians point their puny objectors to their example, and pray that they may have grace to follow in the steps of these noble Christian forefathers, who have left such a precious legacy.

In uncovering these half-buried facts of Revolutionary Church history, while it has been pleasant to describe the noble Christian deeds of the Revolutionary Fathers; it has not been so agreeable to narrate the causes which have led to the unhappy condition of the Protestant Episcopal Church, and to the disastrous events which followed its radical and indefensible change of base.

It has been necessary in presenting Historic Truth, to strip from some noted names of the past, somewhat of the admiration which has been bestowed upon them, but which has not been their rightful due.

Of those who, on the other hand, have deserved higher honor from posterity, the facts we have presented have rightfully vindicated the reputation.

Where unsound doctrines and erroneous practices have been sustained and defended, through the influence of a name which has carried a weight to which it was not entitled, the interests of Gospel truth, and of souls, justifies a full presentation of the facts in the case.

And when individuals have suffered from obloquy and misrepresentation; where there has been a loss of much that was dear to them, as in the case of Bishop Cummins and his friends, surely it was, in view of the verdict of posterity, an imperative duty, to establish beyond contradiction, that the separation from the Protestant Episcopal Church, and the restoration of the Old Revolutionary Episcopal Church, by the organization of the Reformed Episcopal Church; is fully vindicated, and was clearly the work of the Spirit of Truth.

The author has written with the deeper interest from the fact, that for a while he was beguiled by the seductive influence of the exclusive, sacerdotal system, and the Divine Right delusion. He knows by personal experience its effect upon the mind. He has also had extensive opportunity of witnessing its pernicious effect upon others.

He is painfully aware of the immense difficulty of impressing by means of facts and logic, minds that have been narrowed and warped by a slavish submission to authority and tradition. May the Lord greatly bless to those thus affected, the truth here presented in all kindness and love!

M. G.

BROOKLYN, N. Y.
July 4, 1883.

ANNIVERSARY ADDRESS.

DELIVERED IN BOSTON, DECEMBER 3d, 1882.

BY REV. MASON GALLAGHER.

I take great pleasure to-night, on this the ninth anniversary celebration of the organization of the Reformed Episcopal Church, in meeting with our brethren and friends in this old historic city, to which fled as a refuge, two centuries and a half ago, multitudes of brave spirits, who abandoned the old Mother Church of England, for causes similar to those which led ministers and members of the same Communion, planted in this country, to forsake their ecclesiastical home, and to reorganize, on December 2d, 1873, the same Church, with its exclusive priestly hierarchy, curbed and reduced; and its liturgy, deteriorated and defaced by the followers of Archbishop Laud, purified and scripturally revised.

I am reminded, too, by grand historic monuments, that the struggle here commenced for civil liberty, which issued in the establishment of a nation of freemen, who form the beacon-light to all the downtrodden and oppressed people of the world; and whose moral influence in behalf of all that is desirable in national life, far excels in the aggregate, that of any people upon whom the sun has shone. This is not a mere idle boast, for by every sincere advocate of civil and religious liberty, America is admired, respected and loved, in a measure greater than has fallen to the lot of any nation of the past. And all this notwithstanding the many confessed imperfections of a young Commonwealth working out new and untried principles of government.

As an American, the descendant of an Englishman who struggled and suffered on this very ground in securing these transcendent blessings, I claim a right here, on this spot, to recall the scenes, and the Crisis with which this city is so grandly associated; an era, the most important since the Reformation of the sixteenth century.

REFORMED EPISCOPAL SYMPATHY WITH ENGLISH EXILES.

We of the Reformed Episcopal Church, are in the *closest sympathy* with those exiles from the tyranny of Laud, the father of our modern Ritualism, which has compelled us in like manner to forsake the Church of our affections, when corrupted by the same novel, unscriptural devices. We are in sympathy, also, with the brave men, their descendants, who then dared, in weakness, to defy a mighty oppressor, and blessed by Providence, have secured on these shores, forever, freedom from tyrants in Church and State.

Little thanks to the ministry of the Church of Laud and his successors, for those results, and for the blessings which we now enjoy!

That ministry, almost to a man, took part with the enemies of the Revolution. The doctrine of the Divine right of Bishops, was first allowed among professed Protestants, by King James I, in return for the acknowledgment by Bancroft, Laud, and others, of the Divine right of Kings. Both claims are in their intrinsic character, the inherent and essential antagonists of the Divine rights of the people.

They have no legitimate sympathy with the principles and results of the American Revolution. They must be watched wherever they are embraced, and carried out in action; whether in the Church of Rome, or in any other Hierarchical organization.

THE DOCTRINE OF DIVINE RIGHT DANGEROUS.

The bond which links together the ministers and members of the same ecclesiastical organization which has embraced this unreasonable and unscriptural doctrine, of the exclusive divine right of an order of avowed priests, with sole power to convey spiritual gifts relating to the future eternal state, is closer far than that which binds a man to the civil state. It is of an undefined, mysterious nature, breeds superstition, discourages independence of thought, and is the natural foe of free institutions, however it may disguise itself. Fully developed in the Church of Rome, it is the object of anxiety and constant vigilance on the part of the governments of the old world, and in this land forms the source of the greatest danger to our liberties. Any institution among us, which born out of this Papal Corporation, has retained its leading features; an absolving priesthood, and the exclusive Divine right of Bishops, with the denial of a ministry and sacraments to other Protestant Churches, must necessarily remain a sect with limited numbers and influence, spurned by Rome, and the object of distrust to the Communions with whom it arrogantly refuses fellowship.

ITS BANEFUL INFLUENCES.

The religious strife and separations it occasions in households where Christian unity should be especially nurtured; the false views of Christian truth it necessarily engenders; the disrespect it casts upon the work of the Holy Spirit through the agency of devoted and successful Christian teachers, whose position and office it asperses and contemns, while ascribing unreasonable and false prerogatives and gifts to men often vastly inferior in mental and moral qualities; are enough to impel men whose religion is based upon the Word of God alone, to reject and oppose this parasite of Protestantism, the creation of the Stuarts, and of Archbishop Laud. Its proper home is in a monarchical country. In communities where a social and ecclesiastical Caste is allowed, based on something besides brains, character, or learning, it may flourish; but in a land where the Divine right of Kings has been spurned and rejected, the Divine right of Bishops, with its offensive and dangerous adjuncts, has no legitimate place; and as an American citizen, and a sincere, loyal Protestant, I honestly and openly resist it.

THE LAUDEAN BISHOPS THE CAUSE OF THE PURITAN EXODUS.

In divine Providence, we owe to the tyranny of Laud and the Stuarts, the freedom and the independence which now we so greatly enjoy.

If the noble men whom these tyrants subjected to prison, to fine, to mutilation, and other forms of persecution, even to death, had not been driven from the mother country, and their ecclesiastical home, never would there have been reared in this land, a people willing and able to fight for seven years, as the descendants of the Pilgrims did, for the privileges of civil and religious liberty, which, thanks to God and to these patriots, we are privileged now to possess.

In an able article on "The Causes which drove the Puritans from England," the *New Englander* for November, 1882, says:

"It was the bishops who drove the Puritans into Holland; it was the bishops who hung the sword of Damocles over them as they sailed to Plymouth; it was the bishops who compelled the founding of New England, and the great Puritan exodus.

"When fifty years afterwards Archbishop Tillotson and other bishops of England expressed with such energy to Increase Mather, their just resentment to the injury which had been done to the first planters of New England, the old Puritan exclaimed: 'If such had been the bishops there had never been a New England.'"

We may with equal justice remark: "If the Protestant Episcopal Church had possessed such bishops as Tillotson, Burnet, Stillingfleet, Tennison, Patrick, and their associates, Bishop Cummins and his friends would not have been compelled to sever their ecclesiastical ties, and to organize the Reformed Episcopal Church.

THE PATRIOTISM OF THE NON-EPISCOPAL CLERGY.

The same spirit which led the Puritans, under Elizabeth and James, to struggle and suffer for freedom of conscience, and for the unadulterated truths of Holy Scripture, animated the Congregational, Presbyterian, Dutch, and Lutheran pastors of the Revolution, and were it not for their incessant, stirring, patriotic appeals from the pulpit and the rostrum, and their presence in the army, where they both fought and prayed, I feel assured that the War of Independence would never have issued in the success of the Colonists. I am aware that there were noble exceptions to the course of the Protestant Episcopal Clergy in espousing the cause of the mother country. The names of Bishops White and Provoost, Dr. William Smith of Philadelphia,

Peter Muhlenberg, and Dr. Griffith, (Bishop-elect) of Virginia, and Robert Smith of South Carolina, afterwards a bishop, were foremost among those who sympathized with the struggles of the patriot army; while Bishop Seabury of Connecticut, and his disloyal friends were exiled or imprisoned for giving aid and comfort to the oppressors of our grandsires.

THE PRAYER BOOK OF 1785 THE WORK OF THE PATRIOTS OF THE REVOLUTION.

But it is eminently fitting for us Reformed Episcopalians to remember, and for me, on this anniversary occasion, to remind you, in this city of Revolutionary fame, that Bishops White and Provoost, with Dr. Wm. Smith. and Dr. Griffiths, were among the framers of the Prayer Book of 1785, (a Book associated with the names of William III., and his galaxy of Reforming bishops,) on whose principles this country first received its Episcopacy, and on which our Communion, the true, legitimate, *Protestant* Episcopal Church is based; while Bishop Seabury, a non-juror in principle and orders, and a pensioner of the British Government till his death, has impressed his principles of Episcopal and Sacerdotal exclusiveness, and of Sacramental, mechanical grace, upon the Liturgy and Rites of the Church we have been forced to abandon.

That there is a noble body of sound and intelligent Christian men still remaining in that Church, we well know; but that they are tolerated, and that they have received fair and courteous treatment in Conventions, of late, and only within a brief period, is owing to the fact that there is with us, for them at all times, a welcome, safe, and peaceful haven and retreat from their inconsistent and uncomfortable alliance with men in whose principles they have no confidence, and with whose measures they have no sympathy. Sooner or later the separation of these antagonistic elements must occur. We rejoice that the main work has been accomplished, and though the inauguration of the first pure, Liturgical, Episcopal Reformation occasioned the early demise of our beloved leader, who had the grace and courage to effect it, *it is done for all time;* to the glory of God, in the spread of the truth, and to the great comfort and joy of many of the Lord's children.

THE PATRIOTIC OPPOSITION TO HIGH CHURCH EPISCOPACY, AND ESPECIALLY TO BISHOP SEABURY.

It is well known that the fear of the Establishment of an Episcopal Hierarchy on these shores, was one of the causes which led the Colonists to desire separation from the mother country. The inherent nature of this intolerant system was thoroughly appreciated by the descendants of those who had so greatly suffered by it.

The diocese of South Carolina united with the other dioceses on the condition that no bishop should be placed over them. It afterwards elected Robert Smith, who had served as private in the siege of Charleston.

The conventions of Virginia were at first presided over by a layman.

It is well known, also, that John Jay and James Duane, with Provoost and others, earnestly endeavored to prevent all ecclesiastical connection with

Bishop Seabury after the Revolution. But these wise patriots were overpowered by the insane passion for uniformity, and a hollow, unscriptural unity, which has been the bane of the Protestant Episcopal Church.

The Seabury leaven of Sacerdotalism, exclusive Divine right and sacramental grace, was allowed admittance. The Prayer Book of 1785 was essentially changed. The Romish alterations of Elizabeth and Charles were reintroduced. The leaven has spread through the lump, and most significantly, though White survived Seabury a generation, the latter has thoroughly supplanted the patriotic Low Churchman, as the acknowledged Father of that Church, among those who control and direct its affairs, and wield predominating influence therein.

It is, moreover, worthy of note, that in the city where the patriotic White and Smith labored, our Church has been most kindly welcomed, and has widely flourished; while in the metropolis where the principles of Seabury and his followers have long had predominating influence, the soil has been unfavorable and uncongenial to the spread of a legitimate, Reformed Episcopacy. That in this community, so long favored by the influence of the Apostolic Griswold, there is a future of great prosperity to our Communion, there is ample reason for most encouraging hope.

By a singular coincidence, the grandson and namesake of Bishop Seabury, an honest, able and learned sacerdotalist, more than any other man, impressed the principles of Laud and the non-jurors upon the minds of his generation, as those principles have been revived and powerfully set forth by Newman, Pusey, and other writers of the Oxford Tracts. At the time the writer was a student at the General Theological Seminary in New York; the friend and biographer of Bishop White; and the most able and voluminous commentator on the Scriptures which his Church has produced, were the Senior Professors. But they were powerless to resist the overflowing tide of the Oxford delusion under its able American champion. Four of the writer's classmates, with other students, joined the Church of Rome. The money donated by departed benefactors for the education of youth in Protestant principles, has been there largely diverted in the sending forth religious teachers, the open opponents and aspersers of the doctrines of the English Martyrs.

In like manner the munificent bequest of a member of the Protestant Reformed Dutch Church has been perverted, in the same city, to the open, public propagation of semi-Romish doctrines, which would have been most offensive and abhorrent to the benevolent departed donor.

Such sad perversions of religious trusts must necessarily check bequests on the part of Protestant Episcopalians, for they know not but that their legacies may be used in the process of instilling the most unscriptural views in the minds of their descendants, and in the sanctuaries where they have themselves worshiped.

TRUTH NECESSARY FOR UNITY THE DOCTRINE OF THE REFORMERS.

This system blossomed into Ritualism, allowed and extensively embraced in the Protestant Episcopal Church, resisting all efforts to suppress or eject it, has compelled us, as true Protestants, holding the doctrines of the British Reformers, to come out and sever our connection with a religious Body thus proved powerless to oppose error.

At much cost, but with the approbation of conscience, and fidelity to the Truth, the whole Truth, and nothing but the Truth, here we stand. We could not do otherwise. We commit the matter to Him who has led us. "If this counsel or this work be of men, it will come to naught; but if it be of God, ye can not overthrow it."

That the principles of the English Martyred Reformers were in entire antagonism to those which have pervaded the Protestant Episcopal Church with respect to the comparative importance of unity and sound doctrine, is clear. Said Latimer to Ridley: "Hilary saith, 'The name of peace is beautiful, and the opinion of unity is fair; but who doubteth that to be the true and only peace of the Church which is Christ?' St. Paul, when he requireth unity, he joineth straightwithal 'according to Jesus Christ,' no further. Diotrephes, now of late, did ever harp upon Unity, Unity. 'Yea,' quoth I, 'but in verity, not in Popery. Better is a diversity than a unity in Popery.'" Ridley testifies: "As for unity, the truth is, before God I do believe it and embrace it, so it be with verity, and joined to our Head, Christ, and such one as Paul speaketh of saying, 'one faith, one God, one baptism.'"

John Bradford, of equal fame, writes: "The Word alloweth not the more part, but the better part. It alloweth not unity except it be in verity. It alloweth no obedience to any which can not be done without disobedience to God."

Such views are altogether antagonistic to the course of a Communion which allows the views of Colenso at the one extreme, and those of Pusey at the other, and all views intermediate, to re-echo from her pulpits; while those who hold to the plain doctrines asserted by these martyrs, are held in light estimation, and for years have been barely tolerated.

THE REFORMED EPISCOPAL CHURCH UTTERLY REJECTS THE DOCTRINE OF EPISCOPAL DIVINE RIGHT.

Our Reformed Episcopal Church has utterly abandoned and cast out this excrescence on the Church of an Episcopacy of exclusive Divine Right, which logically developed into the Papacy, produced there the Inquisition and other abominations, and which, nurtured in the Church of England, exiled the Puritans; drove out of their pulpits two thousand able, devoted, conscientious ministers; persecuted the Methodists, and compelled them to organize that great and successful Communion which now outnumbers the Church they were forced to leave, and has a far brighter prospect for the future. Here reproduced in this land, the same Episcopal Communion has cultivated Church exclusiveness; suppressed all attempts at simple scriptural reform; discouraged sympathy and union with Protestant Churches; recognized the ministry of Rome, while utterly ignoring that of the Reformed Communions;

favored a return to Pre-reformation principles, and after imperiously and flatly rejecting the petitions of numbers of its most intelligent, devout and respected adherents to return to its original principles, compelled them at last to sever their long and intimate Church ties, and go out, like Abraham, into a new home, followed by the deposing curse of their harsh, unsympathizing parent, but led by conscience and the Spirit of God into fairer pastures and by stiller waters.

As one who has undergone this experience, after earnestly serving that Communion for twenty-seven years, I feel, dear brethren, a deep sympathy with the spirits of the past, who felt much as we have felt and suffered much as we have suffered. Truly, where our afflictions have abounded, our comforts and joys have much more abounded. Brethren, we have had our mission to accomplish, and I thank God heartily that He has counted us worthy thus to labor and suffer for the truth; to be exposed to obloquy and contempt; to encounter the sneer and the sarcasm of those with whom we were formerly associated. To belong to a religious institution in this age, where there is *any self-denial demanded* or *persecution endured*, is truly a mark of Divine favor; what are we that God should bless us so highly? I have considered, when bishops claiming exclusive Divine right, have likened us to refugees in the Cave of Adullam, and when our noble leader was the object of calumny and vituperation, that the hunted chief of that band of outcasts was *the Lord's Anointed*, and came forth in due time to claim and receive the crown of the nation? Let every Reformed Episcopalian look back on such scenes in the Church's history, take courage, be comforted, endure and march on to final, assured victory.

DEPOSITION FROM THE MINISTRY FOR CONSCIENCE' SAKE BORROWED FROM THE PAPAL COMMUNION.

It is right here to affirm that those who established the Reformed Episcopal Church had faithfully served the Communion which they were forced to leave. In attainments and efficient work they were fully up to the average of their former associates, and candid men among the latter have publicly acknowledged the fact. The strange character of the religious organization here arraigned may be gathered from the fact that your speaker, after organizing three parishes, and building as many churches; and after having gathered the largest Sunday-school in his diocese, and presented the largest class for Confirmation known in its history; unchanged in his doctrine, unassailed in reputation, was with his brethren *publicly deposed from the ministry.* And for what cause? For simply doing what the Founder of Christianity and the Reformers of England did: conscientiously seeking to purify and reform the Church which they loved and had faithfully served, appealing to the Word of God alone. They ceased to co-operate with those who, uncharitably and persistently, refused to effect a scriptural reformation. In all these cases of unjust treatment the spirit was the same. Church organization and Church forms were apparently regarded as more important than conscientious scruples or adherence to God's Word. In none of these cases were the ecclesiastical censures approved and ratified in heaven; and it is sufficient compensation for the great trials incident to such conscientious acts, that Reformers now are in full sympathy with those who have preceeded them. For history and eternity will assuredly justify their action. We joyfully abide their verdict. But what of the position of those who, by ecclesiastical fellowship, countenance ecclesiastical oppressors in their unchristlike, uncharitable treatment of their brethren? Countenancing by organic connection those whose doctrines they repudiate as unscriptural, and by remaining in such relation, participants in the action by which men whom they acknowledge as preachers of a sound Gospel, are publicly stripped by a spiteful and inane enactment of their ministerial commission.

No professed Protestant Communion but the Protestant Episcopal assumes to deprive of ministerial authority, those who depart from its ministry to other folds.

It is one of the Roman Catholic peculiarities which this denomination has persistently retained.

In marked Christian contrast to this presumptuous proceeding, Bishop Cummins dismissed a Protestant Episcopal minister who joined the Reformed Episcopal Church, when he returned to his former fold, with kind and courteous words. The Church of England has wisely refrained from such depositions. While such vindictive acts have no validity and are generally esteemed for what they are worth, they are to be regretted for their effect in increasing prejudice against the Gospel.

The P. E. Church presumes to depose from the ministry of *the Church of God*, not simply from its exercise within their own bounds. I have known officials to seek to prejudice the minds of others against Bishop Cummins and his friends on the ground of their being *deposed ministers*. It is the fear of this impious and futile action which has prevented some timid minds from joining our Communion.

BOSTON A GRAND FIELD FOR THE REFORMED EPISCOPAL CHURCH.

I am not suprised at the advance of our *Church in this city*, under the acceptable and faithful pastorate of our beloved brother. The seed was sown here by a wise and godly man. Brother Cutler laid the foundations deep and strong in faith and prayer, and he, who now as a wise master builder is continuing the work in this grand field, is enjoying the savor of the influence of that man of God whose unflinching testimony in behalf of this Church; whose severance, in his declining years, of his deeply rooted ecclesiastical ties; and whose treatment by that Communion, when refusal was extended to his funeral rites in the church edifice where he had officiated with the Divine blessing for a generation; preaches a sermon in behalf of the necessity of our work and our providential mission, more forcible and convincing than any words that I can utter. Strengthened by the sympathy and prayers of so many devoted Christians of all names, with the enjoyment of the Divine blessing, this Church will surely advance to its completion, and ere long the top stone will be laid with shoutings of "grace, grace unto it."

THE MYSTERIES AND MISERIES OF PROTESTANT EPISCOPAL DEPOSITION.

NOTE.—When the bishop, according to the Canon, has authoritatively erased the name of a clergyman from the list in the presence of witnesses, and thus officially deposed him, as far as his Communion possesses the power, from the ministry of the Church of God, information is forwarded to every other bishop of the Protestant Episcopal Church.

The Canon reads, XXXIX, 1832: "When any minister is degraded from the Holy Ministry, he is degraded therefrom entirely, and not from a higher to a lower order of the same. Deposition, displacing and all like expressions, are the same as degradation. No degraded minister shall be restored to the ministry.

Whenever a clergyman shall be degraded, the bishop who pronounces sentence shall, without delay, give notice thereof to every minister and vestry in the diocese, and also to all the bishops of this Church, and where there is no bishop to the standing committee."

It will be seen from the above Canon that the act of deposition is widely published. In addition, the transaction is announced in the bishop's annual address.

It matters not whether the clergyman in his announcement of his determination to withdraw from the Protestant Episcopal Church and ministry, at the same time states that he acts from conscientious reasons, and designs exercising his ministry in another communion; the deposition is absolute.

One bishop speaks of it: "as the inflicting of the irrevocable sentence of displacing or degradation from the ministry."

The Canon appears to be framed with the design of preventing all such conscientious acts, by the stringency of its conditions and the fearful severity of its language. It necessarily acts with great power on the common timidity of the clerical mind, under Episcopal supervision.

The writer when withdrawing from the Protestant Episcopal ministry in 1871, gave his reasons in full for his action, and his design to fulfill his ministry in a field outside of the Protestant Episcopal Connection.

His bishop courteously requested him to give the matter a week's further consideration. But as he had patiently waited for years for that Communion to remove the burdens which had been weighing for a long period on many consciences, and the prospect of relief was entirely hopeless, the step was taken with the fullest deliberation, and the experience of twelve years has fully satisfied him that it was wisely done.

Recently, while looking at the Catalogue of the General Theological Seminary where he received his education for the ministry, the writer noticed among the names of the alumni, his own, with these words appended, "Deposed in New York 1871." Two of his class-mates, who joined the Church of Rome, have the same addenda to their names, and two others of the alumni, one now a bishop of Rome, the other a Roman vice-chancellor. He noticed also two "deposed" alumni who had joined the Reformed Episcopal Communion, and whose career since their deposition, has been largely attended with the Divine blessing on their ministry. There is nothing to indicate to the reader for what cause the deposing curse was inflicted, whether for carrying out the Seminary teaching, logically, and landing in Rome; or for conscientious reasons joining a thoroughly Reformed Communion; or, for moral delinquencies.

The commonest principles of justice and charity find no place in the case of any who leave the Protestant Episcopal ministry. That Communion acts upon the principle and with the spirit of the mother Church of Rome, from which it came out, and from whose medieval errors it has not yet freed itself. One who had abandoned the Protestant Episcopal ministry was asked the reason for his action, "Because," he said, "the conscience is not cultivated in that Communion." This was a very severe charge, but entirely just with respect to the course of that Church in the matter of deposition. For it practically teaches that it is a greater offence to exercise ones ministry in another Communion, with a pure conscience, than to remain a Protestant Episcopal clergyman with that Divine monitor silenced with respect to errors of confessed magnitude. The inference too may be justly drawn from such ecclesiastical action that the call of the Lord Jesus Christ, through the Holy Spirit, is of less importance, and of weaker obligation, than that of the Church through its human officials.

Thankful should we be that there is at last a Church which, while it is Liturgical and Episcopal, is at the same time Scriptural, Charitable, Protestant and Free!

Notes to Anniversary Address Delivered in the Reformed Episcopal Church, Boston, December 3d, 1882.

The Protestant Episcopacy of the Revolutionary Patriots.

BY REV. MASON GALLAGHER.

It has been seen from what has preceded that the circumstances attending the organization of the Protestant Episcopal Church in 1785, were of deep interest from the character of the men who were engaged in the work. Their enterprise was hallowed by the savor of the Revolution in which they had taken a prominent part, and had greatly suffered.

That their task was delicate and difficult all know. With few exceptions the clergy of the Church of England had taken an active part in behalf of the mother country. Most of them had been compelled to leave the country. The few who remained, protected by English bayonets, had written and preached, and prayed for the success of George III. Here and there was one who realized the nature of the struggle, and the vital principles of liberty and justice which were involved. These at the risk of an ignominious death, stood firmly with their ministerial brethren of other denominations, and largely aided in securing the grand result.

And though the good work they effected in establishing their Church on free and broad and liberal principles, was overthrown by the admission in later years of the men who had labored to keep the colonists in a disgraceful submission to a tyrannical King and Parliament, still it is our part as free, enlightened American citizens, and intelligent Christians, to honor their memory, and as Reformed Episcopalians, a century afterwards, to take up their work and to carry it forward to a successful and beneficial result. Claiming as we do, to hold their principles as opposed to those who sympathized with them, neither politically nor ecclesiastically; it is our part to recall the services they rendered as Christians and patriots.

THE MOST PROMINENT ACTORS.

The clergymen pre-eminent in the work were Dr. William Smith and Bishop White of Philadelphia, Bishop Samuel Provoost of New York, Dr. David Griffith, Bishop elect of Virginia; Bishop Robert Smith of South Carolina; and Dr. Charles H. Wharton of Delaware.

Among the Laity were James Duane and John Jay of New York; Richard Peters and Francis Hopkinson of Pennsylvania; John Page and Cyrus Griffin of Virginia; Charles Pinckney and John Rutledge of South Carolina. These are national and imperishable names.

There were others of distinction: Edward Shippen and Thomas Hartley of Pennsylvania; David Brearley and John Rutherford of New Jersey; Jacob Reed and John Parker of South Carolina; Sykes of Delaware. These and other noble spirits were associated with the grand Revolutionary heroes I have enumerated, in organizing the Protestant Episcopal Church as a truly free, Scriptural, American Communion.

PREDOMINANCE OF LAYMEN.

It is eminently worthy of remark, that in the four primary Conventions in which Bishop Seabury was neither allowed presence nor influence, *the lay element largely predominated.* In all the suceeding Conventions *the clergy were in the majority.*

In the First Convention, which settled the Prayer-Book of 1785, three-fifths of the body were laymen. In the Convention of 1789, which decided to admit Bishop Seabury, three-fifths of the number were clergymen. While the power of *the laity* was in the ascendent, the Church was Protestant and Scriptural in its services. As the *Priestly influence* became more general the Communion became naturally more sacerdotal, sacramental and exclusive.

The Church thus, in its infancy, was identical with the Reformed Episcopal Church. *Our Reformation* is simply a *Restoration;* a return to the principles of the patriots of the Revolution.

In like manner as the fathers of our Protestant Episcopacy in America, severed their connection with the mother country, when it departed from its Constitutional principles of Anglo-Saxon freedom; on similar grounds with equal right and justice, Bishop Cummins and his friends separated from the Protestant Episcopal Church when it went back on its founders and departed from its original free, Biblical, Constitutional principles.

We have no doubt that as light is diffused within the P. E. Church, with respect to its own history, that American laymen who partake of the spirit of the American Revolution, will in time, decide favorably as to the claims of our Reformed Communion on their respect, affection and support.

BISHOP WHITE.

In a brief notice of the men who laid the foundations of American Protestant Episcopacy, Bishop White naturally claims prominent attention. To the cause of the colonists, Bishop White's attachment was intelligent and uncompromising. While his friend Rev. Dr. Duche, returned to his former allegiance, Bishop White was firm to the end. An incident which occurred illustrates the risk which clergymen who became revolutionists were aware they incurred.

While Bishop White was taking the oath of allegiance after the Declaration of Independence, an acquaintance made a significant motion of his hand at his throat. Said the Bishop to him afterwards: "I perceive by your gesture, that you thought I was exposing myself to great danger by the step I have taken. But I have not taken it without full deliberation. I know my danger and that it is the greater on account of being a clergyman of the Church of England. But I trust in Providence. The cause is a just one, and I trust will be protected."

When appointed chaplain by Congress at the period of deepest gloom during the Revolution, he at once proceeded to Yorktown to discharge the duties of his office. When the British evacuated Philadelphia he was the only Protestant Episcopal clergyman who remained in the State.

With regard to the organization of the P. E. Church he was connected with every step of the undertaking. He presided in the Convention of 1785, was Chairman of the Committee to publish the Prayer Book, was the first to read it in public service; was consecrated Bishop February 4th, 1787, and preached the sermon at the Convention of 1786.

BISHOP WHITE A LOW CHURCHMAN.

Though Bishop White assented in 1789 to unite with Bishop Seabury and the New England clergy, his ecclesiastical principles were widely different from theirs. With regard to Episcopacy, he held the views set forth by the Reformed Episcopal Church. In his work entitled: "The Case of the Episcopal Church Considered," he writes: "The opinion that Episcopacy was the most ancient and eligible, but without any idea of Divine right in the case, this the author believes to be the sentiments of the great body of Episcopalians in America, in which respect they have in their favor, unquestionably, the sense of the Church of England, and as he believes, the opinions of her most distinguished prelates for piety, virtue and abilities."

His view was also moderate with regard to the Sacraments. When Bishop Seabury pressed the Scottish Oblation service upon the Convention Bishop White most unwisely yielded. In his memoirs, p. 187, he says: "That change lay very near the heart of Bishop Seabury. For himself, without conceiving with some, that the service as it stood, was essentially defective, he always thought there was a beauty in those ancient forms, and that there was no superstition in them. If indeed they could have been reasonably thought to imply, that a Christian minister is a priest, in the sense of an offerer of sacrifice, and that the table is an altar, and the elements a sacrifice, in any other than figurative senses, he would have zealously opposed the admission of such unevangelical sentiments as he conceives these to be."

As Bishop White died just as the Oxford Tracts were beginning their work of un-Protestantizing the Church of England, he did not see the outcome of allowing such language in the Prayer-Book. This ardent Revolutionary patriot sympathized with the views of those who framed the Book of 1785, and though he allowed himself to be overcome and outwitted by the High Churchmen around him, had he lived to this day, he would have been an outspoken and earnest antagonist of those errors which have occasioned the establishment of the Reformed Episcopal Church.

For what he suffered for his Country, for what he did for Christianity, let us honor him. That he failed to see the consequences of his concessions to the urgent and fiery spirits around him, was an error of his head, and not the fault of his loving, patient, conciliatory, pure and honest heart.

PROVOST WILLIAM SMITH OF PHILADELPHIA.

Dr. William Smith, Provost of the University of Pennsylvania, had as prominent a part in establishing the P. E. Church as Bishop White. As an accomplished Theologian and a voluminous and eloquent writer he excelled all his associates. The Convention of 1789, requested him to publish his sermons, and endorsed his sentiments. He was a member of the Conventions of 1785,-86,-89. When the service of the New Book was first read, Dr. Smith preached the sermon. He wrote the able preface to the Book. He presided in the House of Deputies from 1789 to 1799. He was Chairman of the Committee for revising the Liturgy. Bishop White styles him "the most prominent clergyman of his Church."

His sermons in behalf of Colonial liberty were widely distributed throughout England. The Tory Governor Tryon called the attention of the authorities to his treasonable utterances. The sublimely eloquent language in which he depicts the coming grandeur of America; his urgent charge to love, and union among all denominations; his clear unfolding of the principles of civil and religious liberty; give great value and attractiveness to his discourses, which remain a rich legacy to the American people.

In his first Convention address, Bishop Cummins quotes largely from the candid and valuable preface of the Prayer Book of 1785, composed by Dr. Smith, and also from the sermon by Dr. Smith on the occasion when it was first read by Bishop White.

There is room but for one extract from his sermons. "How long, alas! how long shall the divided sentiments of Christians be a reproach to their name? How long shall circumstantials prevail over essentials? embittering the followers of the lowly Jesus and inflaming their breasts with a madness even unto death. A sense of this made the mild Melancthon, when he came to die, thank God that he was going to be removed from temptation to sin, and the fierce rage of religious zealots. Surely, my brethren, I will repeat it again. There is greater weight and moment of Christianity in charity, than in all the doubtful questions about which the Protestant Churches have been puzzling themselves and biting and devouring each other since the days of the Reformation. * * * It will not be so much a question at the last day of what Church we were, nor whether we were of Paul or Apollos, but whether we were of Christ Jesus and had the true mark of Christianity in our lives." Vol. II, pp. 63, 540.

DR. CHARLES H. WHARTON.

Dr. Charles H. Wharton was born in Maryland. Ordained a Roman Catholic priest, God opened his eyes, and he embraced the truths of the Bible. He ardently sympathized with the friends of American liberty. He combined great theological learning and wide scholarship with a poetic genius. His tribute to General Washington is among the best poetic productions of the Revolution.

Dr. Wharton was present and active in the Conventions of 1785, and of 1786. He was on the committee to publish the Prayer-Book with Bishop White and Dr. Smith. Bishop White says of him, "In all the important measures relative to the organization of the Church in this country, and especially in the Revision of the Liturgy, his learning, wisdom, and moderation were most effective and valuable."

One sentence from his works will reveal his liberal, loving spirit. "In this country, where the *Christian* is the only established religion, where tests and subscriptions are unknown; where refined speculations are not likely to deform the simplicity or interrupt the harmony of the Gospel, I look forward with rapture to that auspicious day, when Protestants opening their eyes upon their mutual agreement in all the essentials of belief, will forget past animosities, and cease to regard each other as of different Communions."Vol. II, p. 361.

DR. WHARTON'S VIEWS OF APOSTOLIC SUCCESSION.

Dr. Wharton, like all the English Reformers, rejected the doctrine of an exclusive Episcopal succession. We have had no divine in our Church more capable of judging of this question. A convert from Popery, he had given the subject full investigation. The learned Dr. Thomas Hartwell Horne says of him: "I have long had his masterly treaties in controversy with Dr. Carroll, and value them among my choicest books against Popery." Dr. Wharton writes: "The pretence of tracing up the Roman Church to the times of the Apostles, is grounded on mere sophistry. The succession which Roman Catholics unfairly ascribe to their Church, belongs to every other, and exclusively to none. But that portion of the Christian Church is surely best entitled to this claim, which teaches in the greatest purity, the doctrine of the Apostles. . . .

They have not the inheritance of Peter (*says St. Ambrose, lib. 1, de pan.*) who have not Peter's faith." Works, vol. 2, p. 313.

A few lines from the poem alluded to will indicate the patriotism of this learned, liberal-minded framer of the Prayer Book of 1785, a true Reformed Episcopalian. In his introduction he says, "His sole view in penning this epistle was to express in the best manner he was able, the warm feelings of a grateful individual toward the best of men, to whom he, and every American, will, in all likelihood be principally indebted for the establishment of the independence and commercial prosperity of his country."

> "While many a servile muse her succor tends
> To flatter tyrants, or a tyrant's friends,
> While thousands slaughtered at Ambition's shrine
> Are made a plea to court the tuneful nine;
> While Whitehead* lifts his hero to the skies,
> Foretells his conquests twice a year, and lies;
> Damns half-starved rebels to eternal shame,
> Or paints them trembling at Brittania's name;
> Permit an humble bard, great Chief, to raise
> One truth-erected trophy to thy praise.
>
> Great without pomp, without ambition brave,
> Proud not to conquer fellow-men but save;
> Friend to the weak, to none a foe but those
> Who plan their greatness on their brethren's woes;
> Awed by no titles, faithless to no trust,
> Free without faction, obstinately just.
> Warned by Religion's pure and heavenly ray,
> That points to future bliss the certain way,—
> Such be my country! What her sons should be,
> O, may they learn, Great Washington from thee!"

* Poet Laureate.

THE REFORMED EPISCOPACY OF THE REVOLUTIONARY PATRIOTS.

The history of the Protestant Episcopal Church resembles in one respect, that of its mother Church of England. The first six years of the latter, were its purest and best years.

The days of its glory, were those when King Edward was its earthly head, and when Cranmer, Latimer, Ridley and Hooper where engaged in the establishment of the Church and its formularies.

The brightest period in the history of the Protestant Episcopal Church is that of its organization by White and Provoost, Smith and Wharton, and the framing by these divines, of its first and only Protestant Prayer Book, that of 1785.

To a Reformed Episcopalian, the study of both these periods is an investigation of intense interest. He is in full sympathy with these good men, and their measures. He becomes assured that the Communion to which he is attached, is the legitimate successor of the *Protestant* Episcopal Church, which they, with the co-operation of other revolutionary patriots, so wisely established.

The work of both these periods of Ecclesiastical construction, was perverted, respectively, by two individuals, of temperaments somewhat similar. I refer to Queen Elizabeth and Bishop Seabury. Both these characters were equally tenacious of their respective prerogatives, Royal and Episcopal. Both were firm believers in Divine Right; the first in that of Kings, the other equally in that of Bishops. Both by a successful interference changed materially, and for the worse, the character of the Communions in which, respectively, they held the highest offices. Both greatly retarded the reforming work of their predecessors, and infused a Romish leaven into professedly Protestant Institutions, a leaven which neither Institution has been since able to expel. The growth and influence for good of both the Communions referred to, has been greatly and sadly retarded by the unhappy but successful interference of these earnest and strong willed characters.

Of the men who took part in the organization of the Protestant Episcopal Church, and framed its first Prayer Book, I have briefly described three of the most prominent, Bishop White; Provost William Smith, of Philadelphia; Dr. Charles H. Wharton, of Delaware; large minded, and liberal Churchmen, and earnest, loyal American Patriots.

BISHOP SAMUEL PROVOOST.

I proceed with the list of worthies whom the Reformed Episcopalians claim as their rightful ecclesiastical predecessors.

Samuel Provoost, first bishop of New York, for reasons which will appear as we proceed, has not received from his Church the reverential regard to which his memory is justly entitled. Dr. John W. Francis, in his "Old New York," p. 52, writes: "I introduce Bishop Provoost in this place, because I think our Episcopal brethren have too much overlooked the man, his learning, his liberality and his patriotism."

Rev. Dr. Schroeder, Minister of Trinity Church, in his memoir of Bishop Hobart, p. liii, writes: "Dr. Provoost was a man of cultivated mind and manners. His deep interest, and numerous acts of self denial, in promoting the good cause of our civil liberties, and his prominent agency in organizing the Protestant Episcopal Church in the United States, may well preserve his name and perpetuate his memory. The motto of his ancient family escutcheon *pro libertate*, declared at once the sentiments of his Huguenot forefathers, and the feelings which they had transmitted to him, through five generations, from the middle of the sixteenth century to the year 1742, when he was born at New York."

The Evergreen, 1844, p. 199, says: "The character of Bishop Provoost is one which the enlightened Christian will estimate at no ordinary standard."

A graduate of the first class which passed through King's (now Columbia) College, he spent five years in study at Cambridge, England, and was ordained Deacon and Presbyter in 1766. Returning to New York, he was at once chosen assistant minister of Trinity Church. He served the parish four years, when, on account of political troubles, his opinions being utterly antagonistic to those of his clerical associates, and the leading members of his parish, he resigned his position, and on a small farm in Duchess County, awaited the issue of the coming conflict.

THE MAGNANIMITY OF BISHOP PROVOOST.

Dr. Schroeder remarks: "He resolutely refused all preferment that might be attributed to his sentiments, saying: 'as I entertained political opinions diametrically opposite to those of my *brethren*, I was apprehensive that a profession of these opinions might be imputed to mercenary views, and an ungenerous desire to rise on *their* ruin.' He adds, 'To obviate any suspicion of this kind, I formed a resolution never to accept of any preferment during the present contest. Although as a private person, I have been and shall be always ready to encounter any danger that may be involved in the defense of our invaluable rights and liberties.'"

Harrassed by debts, necessarily incurred, without "a salary or income of any kind," his "estate at New York in the hands of the enemy," a "part of his furniture sold to provide the necessaries of life," and prevented by the Constitution of the State, and the Canons of the Church, from entering into any secular employment; this patriotic clergyman spent his time in study, in deeds of quiet usefulness, and in earnest prayers for the success of Washington and his devoted army, and for the triumph of his country.

He declined invitations to the leading churches in Boston and Charleston, and the chaplaincy of the Constitutional Convention of New York.

When the cause of liberty had triumphed, and peace was declared, his sufferings were rewarded. The newly elected vestry of Trinity Church in whose hands the Council of New York had placed the estate of that corporation, under the influence of John Jay and James Duane, invited Dr. Provoost to the rectorate.

HIS LEARNING AND INFLUENCE.

No Episcopal clergyman stood higher in influence and position than Dr. Provoost. In accomplished scholarship, it may be safely asserted that no American Bishop has surpassed him, and few have equalled him. In addition to his extensive Theological acquirements, he was an adept in various departments of learning. Dr. Francis remarks: "He became skilled in the Hebrew, Greek, Latin, French, German and Italian languages, and we have been assured he made an English poetical version of Tasso. He was quite a proficient in Botanical knowledge, and was among the earliest in England who studied the Linnean classification."

Of his pulpit abilities, we may form an opinion from a contemporary journal. the *New York Packet*, of November 2nd, 1786, describing his farewell sermon on the eve of his departure to England to be consecrated: "The animated and pathetic manner in which Bishop Provoost addressed his hearers, who, as well as himself, appeared to be greatly affected, will be long remembered by those present."

As regards the impression entertained of his official ministrations, the *New York Journal*, November 27th, 1788, referring to the approaching General Convention, says: "It must afford satisfaction to the friends of Christ in general, and to every Episcopalian in particular, to be informed that under the superintending care of Rt. Rev. Dr. Provoost, Bishop of this State, true religion is daily advanced, and more completely established in every part of his extensive diocese."

With regard to his repute in England, a periodical in that country states: "Dr. Provoost is the most dignified clergyman, and rector of the most influential parish in America." See Historical collections, published by New York Historical Society, 1870.

Elected bishop on the same day with Bishop White, he justly shares with that revered divine, the title of "Father of the American Episcopal Church."

Dr. Francis states, p. 168: "It has been more than once affirmed, and the declaration is in print, that Bishop Provoost as senior presbyter and senior in the ministry, was consecrated first, and Bishop White next, though in the same day and hour, February 4th, 1787. The son-in-law of Provoost, C. D. Colden, a man of veracity, assured me such was the case. If so, Provoost is to be recorded as the Father of the American Episcopate. It is painful to pluck a hair from the venerable head of the Apostolic White, but we are dealing with history."

Although Bishop Provoost was fairly entitled to the precedence in the consecration, the preponderance of testimony on this point seems to be in favor of Bishop White, as Senior Prelate.

The fact remains, however, that at the first consecration of an American Bishop, Dr. Claggett, Bishop Provoost presided, and thus bears the pre-eminence, in the matter of the continuance of the Episcopal succession in this country, and thus also became the father of American Protestant Episcopacy.

It will hereafter be shown, that if the counsels of Bishop Provoost, and those who acted with him, had been followed, a far more successful and happy experience would have attended the Protestant Episcopal Church in this country.

A vastly greater constituency of that Communion would be looking back with grateful memory to his faithful, wise and patriotic devotion, and his consistent adherence to the best interests of his Church.

Bishop Provoost became the chaplain to Congress. At the Convention in 1785, he was chairman of the committee which drafted and reported its "General Ecclesiastical Constitution." He took a prominent part in the revision of the Prayer Book on the basis of the reforming bishops in the reign of William III, the principles of which are so fully and ably stated in the preface, by Provost Wm. Smith.

A NON-JURING CHANGE OF BASE.

The intelligent and patriotic churchmen of New York, adopted that Book and its principles, and in that metropolis it was used until 1789, when through the admission of the non-juring element into the General Convention, and the weak and sad concessions of its members, the noble, Scriptural, Protestant work of the past years was discarded, the Scottish Concordat was allowed to triumph, the sacramental and sacerdotal principles were restored in greater fullness, and a legacy of error, dissension and comparative failure in growth and influence was the result.

From this Convention Bishop Provoost was absent through sickness. Neither Jay, nor Duane, nor Peters, neither Page nor Pinckney, the first revisers, were present, to oppose the sacrilegious re-action. That earnest opposition would have been made by these clear-headed, consistent reformers, to such radical, perverse changes, if present, we must believe, and much of the deterioration would have been prevented. Attention will be hereafter called to the changes that were effected.

In 1788, Bishop Provoost consecrated Trinity Church, New York City. On that occasion, John Jay and James Duane were wardens. In addition to these eminent patriots, there worshiped in that congregation, a noble band. Hamilton, Robert R. and Walter Livingston, John Alsop, Rufus King, William Duer, John Ruthford, Marinus Willett and Morgan Lewis, were among the stated attendants at that Reformed Service, under the instructions of the patriotic Bishop.

A NOBLE EXAMPLE OF REFORMED EPISCOPACY.

Two years later, that same edifice presented a solemn scene at the funeral of Theoderick Bland, a member of Congress and soldier of the Revolution. Washington and the Congress were present. James Madison and Richard Henry Lee were among the pall bearers. Bishop Provoost enters the desk and reads the service, and when this is concluded, what venerable clergyman ascends the pulpit to pronounce the funeral oration? It is Dr. William Linn, Pastor of the Protestant Reformed Dutch Church.

Bishop Provoost like Cranmer of old, and like Bishop Hall at Dort, with the Episcopalians of his day, cheerfully recognized the ministerial commission given by the sister church of that Denomination, whose edifices during the war, had been converted by the royal officers into prisons, hospitals and riding schools.

In their principles and their action, ministers and people at that period were Reformed Episcopalians, and would have remained so were it not for the insidious and deteriorating influences of the re-actionary changes in the Book of Common Prayer. The savor of the Revolution had not yet been lost.

We have not time to dwell on the future history of this patriotic, and truly Reformed Episcopalian.

Saddened by the growing influence of the exclusive and sacramental element in his Communion, "and by many painful domestic and embarrassing official cares," infirm in health, afflicted by the loss of his wife, and of his favorite son, and by the reckless course of another son, Bishop Provoost resigned his Episcopate in 1801.

His active career was at a close. Ten years later, he was called from a bed of sickness, after a paralytic stroke, followed by jaundice, to assist at the consecration of Bishops Griswold and Hobart. No other bishop could be obtained to complete the canonical number required. The Church had not prospered under the Seabury transformation, and it was feared that recourse must be had to England for a renewed supply of the sacred, Apostolic, Episcopal *Depositum*, and a fresh start be made by the unfortunate Communion.

He died in 1815. For twenty years he had not been in sympathy with the prevailing sentiments of his Communion, so antagonistic to the principles upon which, by Jay, and Duane, and Peters, and Griffith, and Robert Smith, and other patriotic churchmen, it had been originally founded. Near a century afterwards, it was graciously allotted to Bishop Cummins to revive the noble and beautiful work, which our patriotic fathers had so grandly inaugurated. Profiting by the sad experience of the past, may the Reformed Episcopal Church carry on the same work with the divine blessing to a glorious and permanent consummation?

In describing the clergymen of the Revolution who laid the foundation of the Protestant Episcopal Church on its original, grand, scriptural, free, American principles, we have called attention to three from the Northern States. Bishop White and Provost William Smith, of Pennsylvania; and Bishop Provoost, of New York. The fourth, Dr. Charles H. Wharton, at that time was a deputy from Delaware. The greater part of his ministry, however, was exercised in New Jersey.

Two others, prominent among the Revolutionary clergy in this work, so interesting to us Reformed Episcopalians as fully sympathizing in their principles and acts, equally deserve a eulogy.

DR. DAVID GRIFFITH, OF VIRGINIA.

Dr. Griffith was born in New York City in 1742, the same year and place in which Bishop Provoost was born. He was married in New York in 1766. In the City of Philadelphia, at the house of Bishop White, he died, while attending the General Convention, August 3rd, 1789. After practicing medicine a few years, he went to England, where he was ordained by the Bishop of London in 1770. In 1771, he became a pastor in London County, Virginia. In 1779, he became rector of Christ's Church, Alexandria, and remained such till his death. For ten years General Washington was his parishioner, as well as his intimate friend.

COLONIAL OPPOSITION TO BISHOPS.

The State of Virginia strongly opposed the introduction of bishops before the Revolution. It is not necessary here to relate how offensive the idea of Episcopal supervision was to the minds of the colonists generally. The hostility was not confined to New England. Nowhere was it more determined than in the colony of South Carolina.

John Adams states: "Where is the man to be found at this day, when we see Methodistical Bishops, Bishops of the Church of England, and Bishops, Archbishops, and Jesuits of the Church of Rome with indifference, that the apprehension of Episcopacy contributed fifty years ago (1815), as much as any other cause, to arouse the attention, not only of the Virginia mind, but of the common people, and urge them to close thinking on the constitutional authority of Parliament over the colonies? This, nevertheless, was a fact as certain as any in the history of North America." Dr. Morse's Annals of the Am. Rev. pp. 197.

The ministers of the synod of New York and Philadelphia, held in concert with the consociated Churches of Connecticut, from 1766 to 1775, adopted resolutions with respect to this determined hostility to the introduction of the English prelacy on these shores. Among the members we have the eminent names of John Witherspoon, Drs. Rodgers and Allison, McWhorter, Caldwell, Tennent, Mather, Bellamy and Brainerd.

In one of their annual letters to their English Brethren, they remark: "The late attempts of the Episcopal clergy among us to introduce an American Episcopate, have given a general alarm to our Churches, who fled from the unmerciful reign and persecution of diocesan bishops in our mother country, to settle in an uncultivated wilderness; the recollection of the cruelties and hardships which our fathers, before this peaceful retreat was opened for them, fills our minds with an utter abhorrence of every species of ecclesiastical tyranny and persecution.

"Besides all this, we can assure you that the Episcopal Provinces of Maryland and Virginia do not appear to desire bishops among them; it is only the request of a few discontented missionaries in the Middle Colonies; the laity of their communion (a few high officers excepted), dread the power of a Bishop's Court as much as any other denomination, and have a high sense of liberty, civil and religious." See minutes of Convention, republished 1843.

The House of Burgesses in Virginia, composed almost entirely of Protestant Episcopalians, in 1771, by a unanimous vote, thank four clergymen by name, "for the wise and well-timed opposition they have made to the pernicious projects of a few mistaken clergymen for introducing an American Bishop, a measure by which much disturbance, great anxiety and apprehension, would certainly take place among His Majesty's faithful American subjects; and that Mr. Richard Henry Lee and Mr. Bland do acquaint them therewith."

The writer here quoted remarks: "The circumstances which we have just detailed, unfortunately produced a coldness between the Episcopalians of Virginia and those of the Northern Provinces." See Prot. Epis. Hist. Col. 1851, p. 156.

James Madison in a letter 1774, testifies to the same predominant feeling: "If the Church of England had been the established and general religion in all the Northern Colonies, as it has been among us here, and uninterrupted harmony had prevailed throughout the Continent, it is clear to me that slavery and subjection might and would have been gradually insinuated among us." Rives' Life of Madison, vol. 1, p. 43.

THE PATRIOTISM OF DR. GRIFFITH.

Dr. Griffith preached before the house of Burgesses in stirring patriotic strains, and entered the army as chaplain, in 1776. His regiment was commanded by Col. Hugh Mercer, who fell mortally wounded at Princeton.

Of Chaplain Griffith's army life we have an interesting incident narrated : "The evening before the battle of Monmouth found the army encamped on Mattapan Creek, near the Court House. Late at night a stranger suddenly appeared before Washington's quarters. He wore no uniform and was instantly challenged. He replied that he was Dr. Griffith, chaplain and surgeon in the Virginia line, on business of great importance to the Commander-in-chief. The officer of the General was called, but refused admittance. Washington's orders were peremptory; he was not to be seen on any account. 'Go and say,' replied the visitor, 'that Dr. Griffith waits upon him with secret and important intelligence, and craves an audience of only five minutes.' The General ordered him to be admitted. Entering the Chief's presence, Dr. Griffith said: 'The nature of my intelligence must be my apology for intrusion upon you at this hour. I cannot divulge the names of my authorities, but I can assure you that they are of the very first order, whether in point of character or attachment to the cause. I warn your Excellency against the conduct of Major General Lee, in to-morrow's battle.' So saying, he withdrew as suddenly as he came."

Lee's treachery in that battle, and Washington's terrific rebuke of him on the field, which was followed by Lee's withdrawal from the service, are well known. *See Independent, Sept. 2, 1880*, article by Rev. Charles H. Woodman. Lossing's Hist. Am. Rev., II, p. 623, states that Hamilton and others were present.

In May, 1785, at the First Convention in Richmond, "when thirty-five clergymen and sixty-five laymen met to consider the question of union as proposed to them," Dr. Griffith was appointed a delegate to the General Convention, which met at Philadelphia in the Autumn. At that meeting he took an active part in framing the Prayer Book of 1785.

At the next Convention in Virginia, he was elected Bishop.

THE LAITY OF VIRGINIA.

Dr. Griffith represented an illustrious constituency. With reference to the Virginia laity, Rives, in his life of Madison, Vol. 1, p. 50, writes: "The vestrymen of that day, we shall find, were the Washingtons, the Lees, the Randolphs, the Masons, the Blands, the Pendletons, the Nelsons, the Nicholas', the Harrisons, the Pages, the Madisons, and other names far too numerous to re-capitulate in detail, which stand among the first on the role of our Revolutionary worthies. In these men, and such as these, were the effective and controlling powers of the Church, for the laity and not the clergy were the rulers here."

So impoverished had the Church become by the War, that the money required for Dr. Griffith's journey to England was not raised by the year 1789, and Dr. G.

finally declined the appointment of Bishop. If Dr. Griffith had been consecrated with White and Provoost, and his life had been prolonged, for he died in his forty-ninth year, he would have been the first bishop, as first elected, and been the Father of the American Church. He might have been its Preserver.

In the sermon preached at his funeral, before the General Convention by Provost Smith, he is thus described: "In the service of his country, during our late contest for liberty and independence, he was near and dear to our illustrious Commander-in-chief. He was also his neighbor, and honored and cherished by him as a pastor and friend. When on the conclusion of the War, he returned to his pastoral charge, and our Church, in these States, in the course of Divine Providence, were called to organize themselves as independent of all foreign authority, civic and ecclesiastical, he was from the beginning elected the chief clerical member to represent the churches of Virginia in our General Conventions, and highly estimable he was among us. He was a sound, noble divine; a true son, and afterwards a father as a bishop-elect of our Church, with his voice always, with his pen occasionally, supporting and maintaining her just rights, and yielding his constant and zealous aid in carrying on the great work for which we are assembled at this time, with Christian patience and fortitude, though at a distance from his family and his nearest relatives and friends, he sustained his short but severe illness."

The loss of such a man in that critical period, to his diocese and to his whole Communion was irreparable.

The death of Dr. Griffith, and the admission of Bishop Seabury and his party, on conditions which radically changed the principles of the primary constitution, and the doctrine of the prayer book of 1785, appears to have discouraged the Protestant Episcopal Church in Virginia. The work of its wisest men had been set aside.

It is true a bishop was elected and consecrated in 1790, Dr. James Madison. He attended but two Convention. His wise moderation was there unavailing.

For twenty-five years, and for nine General Conventions, the Diocese of Virginia was represented by but two clergymen and by one layman, who had renounced the ministry. At four General Conventions no Virginia bishop, presbyter or layman was present.

None of her great laymen had a voice in the action which removed the Church from the foundations upon which Jay, Duane, Pinckney, Peters, Page, Ruttledge, Griffin and Shippen had so grandly established it. It was left to weak and unwise hands to mar the work which had been so nobly inaugurated.

BISHOP MADISON OF VIRGINIA.

Bishop Madison of Virginia was briefly alluded to in the last note. This good and learned man deserves a full consideration in this connection, as he was in full sympathy with the liberal American principles, which characterize the Reformed Episcopal Church, as distinguished from the religious Body, which its founders were compelled to abandon.

*THE LOYALIST CLERGY.

To the anti-revolutionary principles, which were held by the loyalist clergy, through whose influence the constitution and Prayer Book of the original Protestant Episcopal Church were radically changed, we have the testimony of one of the most noted of that company; Rev. Dr. Thomas B. Chandler, rector of St. John's Church, Elizabeth, who retired to England at the beginning of the Revolution. In his "Appeal on behalf of the Church of England in America," Dr. C. writes: "Episcopacy can never thrive in a republican government; nor republican principles in an Episcopal Church. For the same reasons, in a mixed monarchy, no form of ecclesiastical government can so exactly harmonize with the State, as that of a qualified Episcopacy. And as they are mutually adapted to each other, so they are mutually introductive of each other."

THE WISDOM OF THE REVOLUTIONARY FATHERS.

It was the avowal of such sentiments, and the obloquy occasioned by them, that led men like Jay and Duane, and Shippen and Page, and Pinckney, to cast aside the feudal principles of the mother Church, and to frame a constitution imbued with the spirit of the Revolution, and therefore acceptable to a free people.

THE HOSTILITY TO EPISCOPACY.

Bishop White states in his Memoir of Protestant Episcopal Church, page 48, that the opinion was generally entertained, "that Episcopacy itself was unfriendly to the political principles of our Republican Government."

Dr. Hawks in his work on the Constitution and Canons of the P. E. Church, remarks: "The effect of the American Revolution upon the Church, had been to attach to it no small share of odium, and few cared to enroll themselves among the clergy of a Communion, small in numbers, and the object also of popular dislike." The reasons for this we have before presented, and Mr. William B. Reed, an Episcopalian, in an address before the Pennsylvania Historical Society confirms the statement. He says: "Patriotic clergymen of the Established Church were exceptions to general conduct. . . . It is a sober judgment which cannot be questioned, that had independence and its maintenance depended on the approval clearly sanctioned of the Colonial Episcopal Clergy, misrule and oppression must have become far more intense before they would have seen a case of justifiable revolution."

Had the P. E. Bishops and clergy generally been men of the moderation and wisdom of Provoost, Griffith and Madison, these prejudices would gradually have been removed, and the names of the patriotic heroes who had reformed the Church, and revised the Prayer Book for a free country, would have established general confidence, and the result would have been a powerful, numerous and widely influential communion.

THE MODERATION OF BISHOP MADISON.

Bishop Madison who had been elected President of William and Mary College at the age of 28, presided at the first Convention in Virginia, consisting of thirty-five clergymen and sixty-five laymen. Consecrated in 1790—in the House of Bishops, he introduced a remarkable resolution which passed that Body. Bishops Provoost and White, probably voting for it. It exhibits the Catholic nature of the man, and was undoubtedly an index to the principles of his Diocese, which has remained so generally faithful to the charitable and moderate views of its noble founders.

HIS EFFORT TO PROMOTE CHRISTIAN UNION.

"The Protestant Episcopal Church in the United States of America ever bearing in mind the sacred obligations which attends all the followers of Christ, to avoid divisions among themselves; and anxious to promote that union for which our Lord and Saviour so earnestly prayed, do hereby declare to the Christian world, that uninfluenced by any other considerations than those of duty as Christians, and an earnest desire for the prosperity of pure Christianity, and the furtherance of our holy religion, they are ready and willing to unite and form one body with any religious society, which shall be influenced by the same Catholic spirit.

"And in order that this Christian end may be the more easily effected, they further declare that all things in which the great essentials of Christianity and the characteristic principles of their Church are not concerned, they are willing to leave to future discussion; being ready to alter or modify those points, which in the opinion of the Protestant Episcopal Church, are subject to human alterations. And it is hereby recommended to the State Conventions to adopt such measures or propose such Conferences with Christians of other denominations, as to themselves may be thought most prudent; and report accordingly to the ensuing General Convention." Bh. White's Mem. Prot. Epis. Ch., p., 168. Perry's Hist. Gen. Con., p. 80.

Dr. Sprague in his Annals of. Epis. Pulpit, p. 320, writes of Bishop Madison: "At this period his heart seems to have been intensely fixed on uniting as far as possible, all sincere Christians. 'There is no one,' he says, 'but must cordially wish for such a union, provided it did not require a sacrifice of those points which are deemed essentials by our Church; from them we have not power to retreat.' He introduced a proposition to this effect in the General Convention held in New York in 1792; but it met with no favor, and was silently withdrawn."

HIS CHARITABLE EFFORTS DEFEATED.

The House of Clerical and Lay Deputies, which contained few of its original founders among the laity, and none of like eminence, appears to have felt the reactionary influence of the new regime. They rejected the proposition as "preposterous," and it was not permitted to be recorded in the journal.

The same treatment has at times since been extended to the various petitions for relief, from burdens on the conscience, presented by numerous venerable and devoted clergymen and laymen.

Bishop Madison in the remaining twenty-three years of his life, attended but one more General Convention. He found the important educational field to which he had early devoted his deep and varied learning, more congenial.* He was the regularly officiating minister of the ancient church at Jamestown, five miles from his College, and on a salary of only one hundred pounds a year.

BISHOP MADISON AS A PREACHER.

With respect to his pulpit talent, President John Tyler, who had been his pupil, remarks: "Bishop Madison in the pulpit, was regarded in his day as strikingly eloquent; his style was copious and Ciceronian, and his manner strikingly impressive. The deep tones of his voice and its silvery cadence were incomparably fine. It has been my fortune to hear our first and most distinguished orators, as well in our public assemblies, as in the pulpit; but I recollect nothing to equal the voice of Bishop Madison." President Tyler continues in his letter to Dr. Sprague: "It was as President of William and Mary, that the chiefest value of his life was exhibited. The hundreds who went out into the world, the light of his teaching, the great and exalted names which were given to fame by several of those, who under him became the disciples of Locke and Sidney, speak more loudly in his praise than any words I can utter and write. Well may his relative and namesake, James Madison, have said of him in the language quoted by you in your letter that, 'he was one of the most deserving men that ever lived.' I could have said no less of one, the memory of whose virtues is indelibly impressed upon my heart and mind—*Exemplar vitae morumque.* As such I regarded him when living, and as such I cherish his memory, now that he is dead." Sprague's Annals, p. 323.

As a specimen of the earnestness which characterized Bishop Madison's addresses to the clergy, Dr. Sprague gives the following extracts: "I do not think that I should discharge my duty in the manner which my conscience and my inclination dictate, were I not to speak upon this occasion with all that plainness and freedom which the importance of the subject demands.

I know that our Church is blessed with many truly pious and zealous pastors,—pastors from whose example the greatest advantage might be derived by all of us; but at the same time I fear that there is too much reason to apprehend that the great dereliction sustained by our Church has arisen, in no small degree, from the want of that *fervent Christian zeal* which such examples ought more generally to have inspired. Had the sacred fire committed to our trust been everywhere at all times cherished by us with that watchful and jealous attention which so holy a deposit required;— had it been thus cherished, might not the ancient flame which once animated and enlightened the members of our Church, still have diffused its warmth ? * * * * What minister, what priest, what bishop is there, who will not, with pious awe, reflect most seriously upon the momentous charge committed unto him; and while he profoundly meditates upon the extent of his duties, ardently supplicate at the throne of grace the renewal of that fervent zeal without which the great ends of His ministry can never be accomplished."

It is due to us Reformed Episcopalians, to give rightful honor to this first bishop of Virginia, who like Provoost, was more eminent for learning and charity, than for ecclesiastical partizanship, and arrogant, sectarian exclusiveness. His fame, as his history is more fully known, as an eminent Christian scholar and educator, will shine like that of Arnold and Wayland, and Muhlenberg, with ever increasing lustre.

THE ACTION OF SOUTH CAROLINA.

We enter upon an intensely interesting theme when we refer to South Carolina and her relation to the American Revolution. The names of her magnificent heroes Marion, Sumpter, Pickens, Moultrie, Laurens; of him who lead them on to final victory, Greene, the beloved and trusted of Washington; together with the Pickneys and the Rutledges, rise up before us to arouse our highest admiration for patriotism, valor, and virtue exhibited in their highest possible perfection.

And when we state that Robert Smith, first bishop of South Carolina, served under these leaders as a private soldier, in the Siege of Charleston, and that the honored names of Pinckney and of Rutledge are associated with his in the formation of the first Prayer Book and the first Constitution of the Protestant Episcopal Church, so radically, so unwisely, and so needlessly changed in after times, we claim as Reformed Episcopalians, an especial interest in the lives of Carolina's noble Christian Patriots.

No State, except Virginia, was so hostile to the introduction of the Hierarchy from England as South Carolina.

The South Carolina Episcopalians were largely descendants of the Huguenots. Their ancestors had been driven from their native country, after the massacre of St. Bartholomew, by the influence of merciless bishops. The Protestantism of the descendants of these martyrs and confessors was not of the later German-silver variety but had the ring of the true metal.

The brave officers who won the battles in the Carolinas were largely Christian men—Generals Morgan and Sumpter who commanded at the Cowpens; Colonels Campell, Williams, Cleveland, Shelby, and Sevier, with Major Morrow at King's Mountain; as well as Colonel Bratton and Major Dickson, at Huck's Defeat, were all Presbyterian elders. Marion too was a Christian man. It required such men to face and repair the repeated disasters of those memorable campaigns.

Ramsey, Hist. S. Carolina, ii, p. 38, says; "Great numbers of French Protestants sought an asylum in South Carolina, at different periods, who were Presbyterians." The number of Episcopalians was comparatively small. Dr. Smyth in article, Southern Review on "The Revolution," p. 43, states; "In South Carolina, the great body of the people were non-Episcopalians. Episcopalianism was indeed the established religion, but not, as has been recently affirmed, 'the *predominant* religion.' * * * The establishment of the Episcopalian religion in South Carolina was the act of a small minority—obtained surreptitiously,—by surprise,—and by a majority, even then of only *one* vote. It never expressed the views of the Colonists, and was never regarded otherwise than as unjust, tyrannical, and unchristian."

When, therefore, the invitation was extended to the Episcopalians of South Carolina to unite in the formation of an American Protestant Episcopal Church, the chief obstacle in the way of the project, was the matter of Bishops, as in Virginia. The history of the order had not commended the institution to mankind; its human origin being apparent from its general results. The office can only be safely allowed when curbed and reduced as in the Primitive Church, when the Bishop was simply a presiding Presbyter and belonging to that order. Such was his position immediately after the Revolution, the same as now allowed in the Reformed Episcopal Church, whose Constitution and Prayer Book have been modelled closely after the wise arrangements of the great men of that period, and are consequently truly American, free and safe.

South Carolina and Virginia were extremely cautious in entering upon the work of Ecclesiastical organization. South Carolina came into the Union of the Churches in the Middle, and Southern States on the condition that no Bishop should be appointed over her. The Laity were to have a share in the Councils of the Church, their negative was to give them co-ordinate privileges in matters of ecclesiastical legislation with the clergy. So Democratic were these early assemblies, that in Virginia and South Carolina at the meetings for reorganizing the Church, laymen were appointed chairmen. See *Church Monthly*, October 1865, White's Memoirs, p. 95.

In the Convention of 1785 South Carolina appointed a distinguished delegation consisting of Hon. Charles Pinckney, Hon. Jacob Read, Hon. John Bull and Hon. John Kean. Messrs. Pinckney and Read were enabled to attend. The General Convention of 1786 had as delegates, Hon. John Parker and Edward Mitchel. At its adjourned meeting in October of the same year, John Rutledge, son of the eminent War Governor and statesmen of the same name, and nephew of the celebrated Edward Rutledge, represented the State. Rev. Robert Smith appointed delegate in 1785, was unable to attend on account of the condition of his family. Rev. Henry Purcell, D. D., was representative that year. In the two Conventions of 1786 Dr. Robert Smith was present, to confirm the wise action of the previous year.

ROBERT SMITH OF SOUTH CAROLINA.

Of the distinguished men who thus laid the fair foundations of that Church, we can speak but briefly of the two most eminent, Dr. Smith and Colonel Pinckney, both truly Reformed Episcopalians.

Robert Smith was educated in England, at Cambridge University. He was born the same year with Washington, 1732. He became assistant minister of St. Philip's Church, Charleston, in 1757. He was buried in the cemetery of that Church in 1801. "Mr. Smith, as his predecessors had done, took a deep interest in the negro school established under the auspices of the Society for the Propagation of the Gospel in Foreign Parts, and he made it a part of his duty to visit the school and ascertain the proficiency of the children twice a week." Our Reformed Episcopal Bishop who has imbibed the ecclesiastical principles of this Revolutionary Father, as his legitimate successor, has taken up his Gospel work in this department, as in his other Episcopal labors.

"At the seige of Charleston by the British troops under Sir Henry Clinton, Mr. Smith preached as he felt the crisis to require, and encouraged his people by his own example in the defense of their liberties and homes, by going himself into the lines armed as a common soldier." Dalcho's Ch. Hist., S. Carolina, p. 216.

We are not surprised to read that: "Upon the fall of Charleston he was marked by the enemy for persecution; for falling ill shortly after its surrender, and even when his recovery was doubtful he was placed under double sentinels. Banished in 1780 to Philadelphia, he returned in 1783 and labored till his death, largely in education, having established the Academy which afterward became Charleston College." See Sprague's Annals, p. 172.

But troubles came upon the Church in the South, as in the North, by the admission to predominating power and influence of Bishop Seabury and his party, who were imbued with the feudal principles to which our Revolutionary fathers were so uncompromisingly and so rightfully hostile. Dalcho writes, p. 218. "The Church would not so easily (if they would for many years) have joined the General Association of the P. E. Church in the United States, had not Dr. Smith been at this period their principal counsellor and guide."

The Constitution of the Church as originally carefully framed by such first class minds, as Judges Jay, Duane, Shippen, and Peters; Governors Pinckney and Page; Griffin, President of Congress, and Senator Rutherford; in conjunction with Bishop Provoost,

Griffith, the Smiths, Wharton, Bishop White and other noble Christian legislators, was destined to be radically changed and the grand work to be marred and defaced, in order to gratify a band of men who had no sympathy with the principles of the American Revolution, but had earnestly sought to keep the colonists in subjection to an imperious and tyrannical King and Parliament. We do not believe that since Apostolic times, any Christian Church, in its organization has ever been blessed with a more distinguished and competent band of laborers, than those who constructed the ecclesiastical Constitution, whose overthrow it is our painful task to describe in detail.

It was a cardinal principle with Bishop Seabury that laymen had no right to legislate in ecclesiastical affairs.

THE CONSTITUTION RADICALLY CHANGED.

The Constitution as primarily framed read: "In every State where there shall be a Bishop duly consecrated and settled, and who shall have acceded to the articles of this general Ecclesiastical Constitution, he shall be considered as a member of the Convention *ex officio.*" At the next Convention to please Bishop White, upon his motion, there was added to this section, these words: "and a Bishop shall always preside in the General Convention, if any of the Episcopal order be present."

At the primary Convention of 1789, with the design of conciliating Bishop Seabury, the Constitution was changed: "The Bishops of this Church when there shall be three or more, shall, whenever General Conventions are held, form a House of Revision, and when any proposed act shall have passed in the General Convention, the same shall be transmitted to the House of Revision for their concurrence. And if the same shall be sent back to the Convention, with the negative or non-concurrence of the House of Revision, it shall be again considered in the General Convention, and if the Convention shall adhere to the same act, by a majority of three-fifths of their body, it shall become a law to all intents and purposes, notwithstanding the non-concurrence of the House of Revision."

This radical departure from the primary Constitution, in thus erecting a separate deliberative body, similar to the House of Lords, a second order of clergy elected for life, was not a sufficient concession to Bishop Seabury and the Eastern clergy, and therefore an adjourned Convention was held the same year, at which still further and more radical concessions were made, whose disastrous results in South Carolina, Virginia, and other portions of the Church, we shall proceed to relate.

THE PRINCIPLE OF THE PRIMARY P. E. CONSTITUTION.

"It is well known that our Church was formed after the Revolution, with an eye to what was then believed to be the truth and simplicity of the Gospel; and there appears to be some reason to regret that the motives which then governed have since been less operative."

Such was the wise, but mild rebuke administered by John Jay, near three-quarters of a century ago, in a letter to the vestry of Trinity Church, when refusal was made by him to the use of the Institution Office in the parish at Bedford, New York. See Life of Jay, Vol. 1, p. 442.

"This document" writes his biographer, "evinces the same inflexible opposition to assumed authority in the Church, which he had so illustriously displayed to usurpations in the State." It is indeed a memorable document to which we shall refer again in the course of our investigation into the work of the Revolutionary Fathers, in constructing the primary Constitution, and the original Prayer Book of the Protestant Episcopal Church.

As John Jay was the most illustrious architect of that Constitution, and fully endorsed the Prayer Book of 1785, it is interesting to read his statement of the sound principles upon which that grand work was based; principles which have governed Reformed Episcopalians, who are now engaged in restoring the same Christian work, so nobly inaugurated a century ago.

OPPOSITION TO THE EPISCOPATE.

The hostility to "the assumed authority and the usurpations" which had been characteristic of the Episcopal order, which prevaded South Carolina, was equally shared by Jay and Duane, and others at the North.

It was to protect the Church from the encroachment of that Order, that the First Constitution was so carefully framed, and if there had been wisdom and statesmanship in those who assumed to guide the Protestant Episcopal Church, adequate to the undertaking in the years succeeding; that Church might have kept pace in its growth with the nation, whose foundations had been laid by the same hands.

There was good reason for the anxiety felt on the subject of Episcopal domination, by the Episcopalians of Virginia and South Carolina, and by their patriotic brethren in New York.

REASONS FOR ANXIETY.

It was well known that a clergyman of extreme High Church, sacerdotal and exclusive views had been requested by half a score of clergymen in Connecticut, to cross the ocean for consecration, and that such consecration had been conferred by the successors of bishops who had been in open hostility to the authorities of their nation, and had sympathized with and prayed for the restoration of the Popish heir of James II. Their very existence as a sect was based on their opposition to William III., whom the people of England, when wearied with the tyranny and usurpations of their Roman Catholic Monarch, had placed on the throne.

And it was because the King and Parliament of Great Britain had violated the principles of constitutional liberty, re-established in the time of William III., that the colonists in America had revolted, and had been forced to establish themselves as a free and independent nation.

And now the clergyman, the ablest of the company, who in America, had labored to frustrate the plans, and to prevent the success of the Revolutionary patriots, had returned to his country as a ruler in the Church, to shape and fashion the infant Communion according to a "concordat" arranged by those who had conferred on him Episcopal power.

When we consider this marked fact in connection with the deep-seated general hostility to Episcopal rule in the colonies, we are not surprised at the action taken by the Protestant Episcopalians of South Carolina in refusing to accept a bishop for their Church.

TESTIMONY OF JOHN ADAMS.

John Adams wrote to Mr. Niles, February 13th, 1818: "This controversy spread an universal alarm against the authority of Parliament. It excited a general and just apprehension, that bishops and dioceses, and churches and priests, and tithes, were to be imposed on us by Parliament. It was known that neither King, nor ministry, nor archbishops, could appoint bishops in America, without an act of Parliament; and if Parliament could tax us, they could establish the Church of England with all its creeds, articles, tests, ceremonies and tithes, and prohibit all other churches, as conventicles and schism shops."

It was the consciousness of the general feeling which had prevailed with respect to Episcopacy, which led Provoost, Jay and Duane, and other patriots to frame their wise, safe and acceptable Constitution.

Before proceeding further with the narrative of the complete abandonment of the principles of this original Constitution, it is proper to call attention to another patriotic bishop of the South, Rev. Charles Pettigrew.

REV. CHARLES PETTIGREW.

In the Appendix to the Life of Judge James Iredell, Vol. II. p. 591, we have the "Biographical notice of the Rt. Rev. Charles Pettigrew, First Bishop of the Diocese of North Carolina." He is thus styled, inasmuch as he was elected to that office, and was faithful in the oversight of the Church in the State. And inasmuch as an honest and fair *election* constitutes a presbyter a bishop; *Consecration* being simply an orderly and seemly ceremony, such as the *Coronation* of a King, not conveying power, already possessed, but affirming it; and moreover as Mr. Pettigrew was received as a bishop of the churches of all denominations, he could justly claim the official title which he so universally received.

He appears indeed to have been more fully a true Scriptural Overseer, than any of his contemporaries. We read that—"During all this period he seems to have been not so much at the head of the Episcopal Church, as of religion in general, for there are various letters to him from Edward Dromgoole, and other Methodists, who either resided in or traveled through that region, and also from Lutherans, &c., giving him an account of their movements, and requesting an attendance at their meetings. Indeed the Church Establishment having been dissolved, and all religious organizations broken down, the enemies of the evil one fought together, with no other bond of union than a common foe."

PETTIGREW A PATRIOT.

"In his politics he was a Whig," that is a patriot. "After the peace he received various invitations from the neighboring parts of Virginia, which were declined."

Born in Pennsylvania, he removed to South Carolina, with his father's family. His father was of Huguenot extraction. His ancestors came to Scotland; from thence emigrating to County Tyrone, Ireland, and from the latter country to America. The father, James Pettigrew, converted under the preaching of Whitfield, abandoned the Church of England. Educated under two Presbyterian ministers, one of them the famous James Waddel, (Wirt's blind preacher): "uniting to a devout spirit a vigorous intellect, and highly respectable mental acquirements: and having returned to the faith from which his father had withdrawn, and to which, for several preceding generations his ancestors had belonged, he determined to devote himself to the ministry." He was ordained by the Bishop of London in 1775.

THE CHURCH IN NORTH CAROLINA.

In 1789 Bishop White suggested to Governor Johnson of North Carolina, the propriety of organizing the P. E. Church in that State. The latter referred the matter to Rev. Mr. Pettigrew, who did not succeed in securing a Convention until May, 1794. On that occasion a constitution was framed and adopted, and Mr. Pettigrew elected Bishop.

"With regard to this honor he sincerely said, *Nolo Episcopari;* the state of his health seemed absolutely to forbid it; but in the depressed state of the Church, and the scattered situation of its ministers, the acceptance of this part was deemed by his fellow Christians a duty, and he yielded. Various alarms of yellow fever at Norfolk and Philadelphia, with their accompanying quarantine, cutting off all communication, prevented him from meeting the General Convention for some years, and in the latter part of his life declining health rendered him unequal to the exertion. Though he was thus unable to put the finishing stroke to the foundation, yet his labors in rescuing the ministers and their parishes from the disconnected state in which they were disposed to continue, and in increasing and diffusing a zeal for religion, were of great service, not only in the cause of the Church, but of Christianity in general." Life of Iredell, II., 592.

HIS ZEAL FOR EDUCATION.

Mr. Pettigrew, like the two neighboring Bishops, Smith and Madison, entered warmly into the matter of education. He was greatly instrumental in establishing the University. Such was his conviction of the importance of the measure, and his zeal for its success, that once being compelled to choose between the General Convention, and a meeting of the Friends of the University, he preferred the latter.

Moore in his Hist. North Carolina, I, 494, writes: "In 1776 not more than six established ministers were to be found in the State. Rev. Charles Earll of Edenton, and Adam Boyd of Wilmington, were devoted Whigs. . . . Bishop Pettigrew won the esteem and confidence of all Christians, and was their earnest co-adjutor in every good work. Edward Dromgoole, the Methodist Missionary, then planting the earliest churches of that faith in North Carolina, and others bore testimony to the noble charity of his creed and practice."

His duties as a minister were very onerous; as he had three or four counties under his charge, and was expected to preach a funeral sermon for every respectable parishioner. He had, also, to exercise his ministry under the disadvantage of a sickly climate. The death of Rev. Mr. Earll cast upon him the care of that whole section.

In 1794 he built Pettigrew Chapel near Lake Scuppernong which he presented to the Church. From this time till his death in 1807, he refused to receive any compensation for his services. "An enlightened, cheerful and consistent Christianity pervaded his whole life, and particularly characterized him in his domestic relations."

AN ELOQUENT AND FITTING EULOGY.

The Edenton *Gazette* notices: "The death of that zealous and venerable disciple of the blessed Jesus, the Rev. Charles Pettigrew, Bishop of the Protestant Episcopal Church in this State, who died at his house in Tyrrel County on the 7th of April last, (1807). To do justice to the character of this pious and excellent man would require talents which we have not the happiness to possess, and far exceeds the narrow limits of this paper. His public ministrations in this place for many years render eulogy unnecessary. His chaste and classical discourses, his fervid and animated devotion, his irreproachable and evangelical life, will long, very long, be remembered with melancholy regret by those who enjoyed the advantage of his public admonitions and instructions. In him were exemplified that 'simplicity and godly sincerity' which are the perfection of Christian character. Oppressed by the infirmities of a feeble constitution and frequent disease, his cheerfulness did not desert him. As the world and its fleeting joys receded from his view his faith in Christ and hope of immortal glory acquired additional vigor. * * * * 'Mark the perfect man and behold the upright; for the end of that man is peace.' "

A TRUE REFORMED EPISCOPALIAN.

We have quoted the greater part of this striking and beautiful eulogium on this true Apostolic bishop, that his memory may receive that veneration from the Reformed Episcopal Church which is his due. In his patriotic devotion to his Country; in his unbounded affection for Christians of all names; in his fraternal intercourse with the Church universal; in his unceasing devotion to the preaching of the Gospel, rather than to human forms of worship; in his successful furtherance of Gospel unity, we justly claim him as a Reformed Episcopalian. He stands forth a beautiful model to all Christian ministers.

While the zealous champions of a boasted Episcopal, Digital Succession, and an undeviating adherence to the phrases of a human Liturgy, are held up to admiration; this eminent man of God, this Revolutionary patriot, this zealous evangelist and successful preacher, like others, has not received from the Communion he so faithfully served, the honored remembrance which is his due.

NEGLECT OF THE SOUTHERN CHURCH.

So much absorbed was the Church in its recent union

with the High Church Loyalists, that its more important interests in other portions of the land were neglected. White, in his Memoirs, p. 172, referring to the application from North Carolina, in 1794, and the failure of Mr. Pettigrew to appear, writes, "Why nothing was done afterwards for the carrying the design into effect, is not known, unless it be the decease of the Reverend person in question, which must have happened not long after." As the bishop-elect survived thirteen years, the want of interest manifested in the matter on the part of the Presiding Bishop, is of a marked character. But the new departure of 1789, had impressed a new character upon the Church.

A general decline pervaded the Church at the South. When at length, sixteen years after the death of the Apostolic Pettigrew, the Church in North Carolina received a new bishop, unfortunately he belonged to the new regime. His views may be gathered from a single paragraph from a sermon—"On the doctrine of Divine right in the ministry, I hold and teach, that it can be derived only from the Apostles of our Lord Jesus Christ, by succession in the Church, through the line of Bishops as distinct from Presbyters; that it is essential to the validity of the Sacraments, and from its very nature incapable of any graduation. It is either Divine right or no right at all." See Bishop Ravenscroft's Works, Vol. 1.

And when a regularly consecrated successor to Ravenscroft was afterwards sent, imbued with Non-juring sentiments, that system was carried out to its logical conclusion, and the bishop landed in the Church of Rome.

In a sermon delivered shortly after the sad perversion of this bishop, Rev. Charles C. Pinckney, of Charleston, S. C., a worthy member of an illustrious family, remarks: "Bishop Ives used to boast that he was a Churchman of the Hobart and Ravenscroft school." We admit his claim; and apprehend that he had only learned too well the lessons taught in that High Church Seminary.

"He rebaptized all who entered our Church from other denominations, though baptized as adults elsewhere; once giving as a reason to the writer that he had no respect for Sectarian baptism. All non-Episcopal bodies he despised, counting the loss of Episcopacy enough to cut them off from God's favor.

"May this fall of one of our bishops, recall to the remembrance of the Church, the warning voice of a wiser, and an older man; with wonderful forecast, Bishop White often protested against misunderstanding the word 'Priest,' in the Levitical and Romish sense. He declares it to be synonymous with 'Presbyter,' and in no wise a mediating, or sacrificing, or absolving officer."

Yet with a strange inconsistency, and inexplicable weakness, to please Bishop Seabury, Bishop White restored the word "priest," after he had banished it from the Prayer Book of the Revolution.

It has been left to the Reformed Episcopal Church, following the example of the English Reformers, and the Revolutionary Fathers, again to eject the fatal word, with other expressions, necessarily promotive of Roman, Mediæval and Anti-Christian errors and practices, as history has abundantly shown.

We are calling attention to the original Constitution of the Protestant Episcopal Church, and to the First Prayer Book as framed by the Patriots of the Revolution; and to the extraordinary and radical changes made a few years afterwards in the grand work of this distinguished company of ecclesiastical legislators.

An account has been given of the more eminent of the clergymen who took part in this important transaction. Of twenty-two who were present in the Conventions, we have noticed the six most prominent, five of whom were bishops or bishops-elect.

The laymen who were engaged in the work of laying the ecclesiastical foundations, which they believed were to be permanent, were forty-two in number, twelve of whom on account of their eminence as statesmen and jurists we shall proceed briefly to describe. In intellect and reputation, as well as fitness for their mission, they were equal, if not superior, to their clerical co-laborers.

DEPUTIES FROM NEW JERSEY.

New Jersey was represented by a very distinguished deputy. Hon. David Brearley served with distinction as Lt. Colonel in the War of the Revolution. He rose rapidly in the legal profession, was appointed U. S.

District Judge, and soon reached the highest honor, that of Chief Justice of his State, which he held for nine years. He is especially deserving of record as being a member of that famous body by whom the Constitution of our Republic was framed. He was also a member of the State Constitutional Convention. No American has held more distinguished positions at such an early age. He died when forty-four years old, ere he had reached the full maturity of his powers.

John Rutherford may properly be noticed among the eminent men of New Jersey, though at the time a delegate from New York. Rutherford, who was a nephew of General Lord Stirling, had served as Colonel in the Revolution. He was Presidential elector for New Jersey on several occasions, and also U. S. Senator. Appointed by the Council of the State a vestryman of Trinity Church, in 1784, and made Clerk of the Corporation, he resigned in 1787, on moving from the State. The thanks of the Board were presented him for "the utmost attention paid by him to the interests of the Corporation, and the duties of his station as clerk." Berrians' Hist. of Trinity Church, p. 185.

THE PENNSYLVANIA DELEGATION.

From Pennsylvania came more than one-third of the entire lay delegations, and among them were men of national reputation.

Thomas Hartley was a distinguished lawyer, a Colonel in the War, and in Congress from 1789 to 1800.

Edward Shippen, a very eminent jurist, after holding many distinguished positions, became the Chief Justice of the State. A biographer thus sums up his character: "As a valuable citizen, an accomplished lawyer and judge, remarkable for the great extent and minute accuracy of his knowledge, he must ever be conspicuous among those worthies who have won, by their virtues and their talents, an imperishable name." National Portraits, Vol. 1.

Richard Peters was Captain in the Revolution, and Secretary of War, from 1776 to 1781. He retired with the express thanks of Congress. Returning as Representative, he served several years, and declining a Fiscal office tendered by Washington, was appointed U. S. Judge, an office which he filled with great distinction for thirty-six years. Lossing writes: "Next to Robert Morris, Mr. Peters was one of the most efficient men in providing the ways and means of carrying on the war. In the summer of 1781, Washington prepared to attack the British in New York, and was expecting the aid of the Count De Grasse, with his squadron of French ships of war. He received notice that De Grasse's aid could not be given. Washington was greatly disappointed, but instantly he conceived the expedition to Virginia, which resulted in the capture of Cornwallis. Peters and Morris were both in Washington's camp on the Hudson. At the moment when he conceived the Virginia expedition he turned to Peters, and said, 'What can you do for me?' 'With money everything—without it, nothing,' Peters replied, at the same time casting an anxious look toward Morris the great financier. 'Let me know the sum you desire,' said Morris. Before noon, Washington had completed his plans and estimates. Morris promised the money and raised it upon his individual security." Mr. Peters superintended the provision and preparation of the necessary supplies for this important and decisive enterprise. "Our Countrymen," p. 170.

EMINENT SOUTH CAROLINAINS.

South Carolina was ably represented in these Conventions. Hon. John Parker was a member of Congress at the time he assisted in founding the Protestant Episcopal Church. Hon. John Rutledge, son of the eminent statesman of the same name, distinguished himself both in the Legislature of his State and in the U. S. Congress. Hon. Jacob Read, a member of Congress, while in the Convention, became U. S. Senator, presided over that body, and for many years held the office of U. S. District Judge. The most distinguished delegate from the State was Hon. Chas. Pinckney. The name of Charles Pinckney is so identified with the era of the Revolution and the Constitution, that it is not necessary here to recall his history. As member of Congress, of the Senate, as a framer of this country's Constitution, and repeatedly Governor of his native State, and as Minister Plenipotentiary, he occupies a pre-eminent position in the national annals. Curtis, in his Hist. of Constitution U. S., 1. p. 486, enumerates him among the "men of great distinction and ability, celebrated, before and since the Convention, in that period of the political history of America which commenced with the Revolution, and closed with the eighteenth century."

VIRGINIA NOBLY REPRESENTED.

Virginia, whose early Diocesan Conventions were resplendent with great Revolutionary names, sent two of her most prominent statesmen to organize the American Episcopal Church.

Hon. Cyrus Griffin, honorably connected with families in England, entered warmly into the defense of the just rights of the colonies, and pledged his life and property on the momentous struggle. He took a distinguished part in Congress, and during the formation of the Constitution, was President of that Body. The unanimity with which he was selected by the Diocesan Convention of Virginia for such a responsible position, indicates the great respect which was felt for his ability and character, by that distinguished assembly.

He was President of the Supreme Court of Admiralty, and Judge of U. S. Court from 1789 to 1810. Washington when appointing him Indian Commissioner styles him "a regular student of law, having filled an important office in the Union in the line of it, and being besides a man of competent abilities and pure character."

GOVERNOR JOHN PAGE.

Hon. John Page, one of Virginia's most noted sons, was among the most efficient and prominent in the work of the Convention. Bishop White's mention of him indicates the active part he took in Committees and on the floor of the House. No one in the Convention, from ability and study of the matters involved, was more fully fitted for the great Christian work in which these master minds were engaged.

Mr. Page's residence was Rosewell, on the York river, one of the most capacious and extensive residences in the State; built by an eminent ancestor of the same name. Jefferson and Page were schoolmates and most intimate friends through life. Howe, in his Historical Annals, describes the two honored statesmen enjoying from the roof of the mansion the magnificent prospect of ten miles in extent, and discoursing on matters pertaining to the welfare of that Nation, which both had been greatly instrumental in calling into existence.

Mr. Page at once embraced ardently the side of the Colonists, and like Cyrus Griffin, risked his great estates and his life on the issue. At an early period, when Lord Dunmore, the Governor, had seized the powder and arms of the Commonwealth in order to cut off the means of military defense, Mr. Page was the only member of his Council who stood out against his arbitrary measures. In his autobiography, Mr. Page writes, "I advised the Governor to give up the powder and arms he had removed from the magazine. But he flew into an outrageous passion, smiting his fist on the table, and saying, 'Mr. Page, I am astonished at you.' I calmly replied I had done my duty and had no other advice to give." Rives' Life of Madison, I., p. 94.

BISHOP MEADE'S EULOGIUM.

Col. Page was with Washington on one of his expeditions against the Indians, and commanded the militia to oppose the invasion of Gen. Arnold. Bishop Meade writes: "He was the associate and intimate friend of Mr. Jefferson at college, and his follower in politics afterwards, though always differing with him on religious subjects, endeavoring to his latest years, by correspondence, to convince him of his errors. He was a zealous friend of the Episcopal Church, and defended in the Legislature, what he conceived, were her rights, against those political friends with whom he agreed on other points. So zealous was he in her cause that some wished him to take Orders, with a view to being Bishop of Virginia. His name may be seen on the journals of the earliest Conventions of Virginia. I have a pamphlet in my possession in which his name is in connection with those of Robert C. Nicholas, and Colonel Bland, as charging one of the clergy in or about Williamsburg with false views on the subject of the Trinity, and of the eternity of the punishment of the damned. His theological library was well stored for that day. The early fathers of Greek and Latin, with some other valuable books, were presented to myself by one of his sons, and form a part of my library. It may not be amiss to repeat what I have said in a preface to the little volume written as a legacy by the first of this name to his posterity,—that seven of them are now ministers of the Episcopal Church, and two who were such are deceased." "Old Churches of Virginia," I. 148. Bishop Meade says further, p. 333: "Mr. Page was not only the patriot, soldier, and politician, the well-read theologian, and zealous Churchman—so that, as I have said before, some asked him to take Orders with a view to being the first Bishop of Virginia,—but he was a most affectionate domestic character. His tenderness as a father and attention to his children is seen in the fact that, when attending Congress held in New York in 1789, he was continually writing very short letters to his little ones, even before they could read them."

In one of these letters Mr. Page writes of New York: "This town is not half as large as Philadelphia, nor in any manner to be compared to it in beauty and elegance. Philadelphia, I am well assured, has more inhabitants than Boston and New York together. The streets here are badly paved, very dirty, narrow as well as crooked, and filled up with a strange variety of wooden, stone and brick buildings, full of hogs and mud."

Mr. Page was one of the most conspicuous members of the Convention which formed the Virginia Constitution; member of the first U. S. Congress, and Governor of the State from 1802 to 1805. He held other public offices till his death in 1808.

President Madison thus warmly eulogizes him: "The memory of Governor Page will always be classed with that of the most distinguished patriots of the Revolution. Nor was he less endeared to his friends, among whom I had an intimate place, by the interesting accomplishments of his mind and the warmth of his social affections, than he was to his country by the evidence he gave of devotion to the republicanism of its institutions." Rives' Life, I. 76.

Pre-eminently competent was this great and good man for the work in which with Griffith and Griffin of his State he was associated, and we may, from a knowledge of the admirable fitness of these remarkable men, appreciate the astonishment and grief with which the Churchmen of Virginia beheld in a few years the summary abandonment and overthrow of their Constitution and Prayer Book, in order to propitiate a few clerical loyalists, of the most extreme ecclesiastical stripe, and therefore doubly obnoxious to liberal-minded patriotic Americans.

THE SAD RESULT.

That the Church in Virginia, staggered by such wholly unexpected and utterly inconsistent action, should have lost hope of success, and ceased further to progress, was the legitimate, logical result of the marvelous blunders of the ecclesiastical legislation of the Conventions of 1789.

It was reserved for Bishops Moore and Meade, men of the stamp of Griffith and Griffin and Page; of Jay and Duane; of Peters and Pinckney, in later years, to recover in some measure, the ground so hopelessly and rashly lost. That Diocese is suffering now from its continued organic connection with a Body hopelessly infected with mediæval error in its Liturgy and Offices, and with feudal principles imbedded in its Constitution and Laws.

If forty years ago, when in General Convention it failed in its earnest efforts to check the irresistible development of the semi-Romish elements within the Church, through the agency of the Oxford Tract movement; it had then asserted its independent, inalienable, Christian rights, and had severed its connection with an organization drifting away from the Word of God, and pure Gospel truth; a nobler, purer, and more extensive Communion would have been the happy result of such a courageous return to the sound doctrine, pure worship, and manly, liberal spirit of the pioneer ecclesiastical architects of the Revolution.

No delegation exercised a more powerful influence upon the General Conventions of 1785 and 1786 than the one from New York.

The position, patriotism, and learning of Bishop Provoost, the exalted services and character of John Jay, the great ability and influence of James Duane, with the attendance of Colonel John Rutherford, vestryman and clerk of Trinity Corporation, who also appeared as a Representative from the same State, contributed greatly to the efficiency and success of the work.

The result was the free, American Episcopal Constitution of which that of the Reformed Episcopal Church is the counterpart. The revision of the Prayer Book on a sound Scriptural and Protestant basis was largely due to these eminent Christian statesmen.

Born in New York city in February, 1732, the same year and month with Washington, and educated for the Law in the office of the eminent Colonial counsel, James Alexander, father of Lord Stirling, Duane was admitted as attorney in 1754. In 1759 he married the eldest daughter of Colonel Robert Livingston, proprietor of Livingston Manor. From this connection, and the large estate inherited from his father, and his own native talent he soon attained extensive practice and influence in his profession. His offices before the war were Clerk in Chancery, and temporarily, Attorney General.

PUBLIC SERVICES OF JAMES DUANE.

The people of New York city and the neighborhood, elected Mr. Duane to the Congress of 1774 when the Colonial authorities refused to act. From the journal of John Adams it appears that Duane was the most prominent man in that delegation. Duane and Jay were appointed to the Committee to state the rights of the Colonies. Duane was re-elected to the Congress of 1775. Recalled home with Mr. Jay to assist in framing a State Constitution, he was thereby prevented with his illustrious co-patriot from signing the Declaration of Independence, passed during their absence. His name is appended to the Articles of Confederation of 1781.

Leaving New York on the 8th of June, 1774, he never returned until he entered it in triumph on the evacuation of the British in 1783. In the same year he served as a Senator in the State Legislature, and also as one of the Council for the Government of the Southern District of New York.

When Duane entered his native city, "he found his houses in King (now Pine) street, and at the corner of Water and Fly streets, almost entirely destroyed. His farm, as he calls it, consisting of about twenty acres, at what is now called Gramercie Park, and its vicinity, was in pretty good order, the house having been occupied by one of the British Generals." Jones' Mem. Doc. Hist. N. Y., IV., 1077.

In 1784, the Common Council petitioned the Governor to make Mr. Duane mayor, "as no one," they say, "is better qualified, so none will be more acceptable to us and our constituents at large than Mr. Duane. Few have sacrificed more or deserve better from their country."

Under him in the Mayor's Court where he presided for six years, were trained to eminence, Hamilton, Burr, Troup, the Livingstons, Hoffman and others. His decisions were all confirmed by the Supreme Court.

During a portion of this period Duane also served as State Senator, and was in the Convention of New York, which adopted the U. S. Constitution in 1788. General Washington appointed him the First District Judge for New York when the new Government went into operation. After holding this office for five years, he retired to his extensive estates at Duanesburgh, where he died in February, 1797.

HIS INTEREST IN CHRISTIAN WORK.

The immense amount of business transacted by Mr. Duane would seem to preclude him from taking part in ecclesiastical affairs, but we learn from Judge Jones that, "no layman of the Episcopal Church was more instrumental than himself in uniting all its members under one Constitution, and in obtaining the Consecration of her first Bishops." Mem. p. 1083.

"We find him taking an active part on the side of the Church * * * * in the disputes about taxation by authority of Parliament alone, when such authority was first exercised. He was a decided Churchman, but like his friends Jay and Chancellor Livingston, he was a strenuous advocate both for civil and religious liberty."

"In 1784, the Council took possession of the property of Trinity Church, set aside an election of vestrymen that had been held just before the Americans regained New York, and ordered a new election, in which Mr. Duane was chosen one of the Church Wardens, and other Whigs, vestrymen. This election was afterwards confirmed by Act of Legislature, and the persons elected chose as rector of the Church, the Rev. Samuel Provoost, a Whig, who had left New York after the British took possession, and who was afterwards the Bishop of the Diocese. The property was afterwards restored, and Mr. Duane continued the elected Church

Warden so long as he remained a resident of the City of New York." Jones' Mem., p. 1077.

In April, 1794, Mr. Duane resigned the Wardenship which he had held for ten years, having been also a vestryman of the Corporation for several years previous to the Revolution. Resolutions highly expressive of respect were transmitted by the vestry to Mr. Duane, through his intimate friend of congenial ecclesiastical and civil views, Bishop Provoost. Before his death Mr. Duane erected a church edifice at his individual expense, which he presented to the parish at Duanesburgh.

THE STANDING AND INFLUENCE OF JAMES DUANE.

His biographer tells us that he was a man of genial nature and much beloved by his friends. This fact comes out incidentally in a letter from Robert Morris to John Jay, written Feb. 5, 1777. Morris was second only to Washington in services during the Revolution. Botta, in his "War of Independence," III. 343, writes of Morris: "The Americans certainly owed, and still owe, as much acknowledgment to the financial operations of Robert Morris, as to the negotiations of Benjamin Franklin, or even to the arms of Washington." In his letter to Jay, Morris writes: "I hate to pay compliments, and would avoid the appearance of doing it, but I cannot refrain from saying I love Duane, admire Livingston, and have an epithet for you if I had been writing to another." Jay's Life I, 66. On October 8th, 1784, at a Convention of Clergy and Laity, while Chancellor Livingston was Warden of Trinity Church, he was appointed Trustee of the Corporation for the Relief of Widows and Orphans of the Episcopal Church, together with Jay and Morris. To the same Board were appointed Duer, Rutherford, Governor Lewis, Hamilton, Alsop, and Walter Livingston, together with Governor Morris, of Philadelphia. In the Convention which appointed them sat Col. Marinus Willett, of New York, and Richard Willing, of Philadelphia. Such were some of the eminent names connected with the infancy of the American Episcopal Church.

With reference to the general view of the conspicuous ability and services of James Duane, we will confine ourselves to the testimony of Alexander Hamilton, himself confessedly the most commanding intellect of his time. Hamilton, in a memorable letter written to Duane while in Congress, in 1780, in which he outlines with extraordinary power the future Constitution of our Country, closes thus: "My dear sir, this letter is hastily written, and with a confidential freedom, not as to a member of Congress, whose feelings may be sore at the prevailing clamor, but as to a friend who is in a situation to remedy public disorders,—who wishes for nothing so much as truth, and who is desirous for information even from those less capable of judging than himself." Hamilton's Life I, pp. 284-305.

It remains to present a notice of John Jay, and then there will be stated the intelligent and earnest efforts of Jay and Duane in connection with Bishop Provoost and others to organize the Episcopal Church on a free, Scriptural, American basis, and to preserve it from the attempts of Bishop Seabury and his party to substitute the feudal, illiberal, and Semi-Romish principles of the Non-Jurors, which have ever proved such a blight to the Church. While interesting, it is a melancholy history full of warning; but at the same time it is satisfactory and strengthening to Reformed Episcopalians to be assured that they are in the fullest sympathy with the great Revolutionary Patriots, whose services to the Church, as well as the State, we have been privileged briefly to notice.

THE MOST EMINENT OF REFORMED EPISCOPALIANS.

We have reserved for the last notice of the founders of the Protestant Episcopal Church of the Revolution, the most eminent of that illustrious assembly of Christian legislators, regarded by many as the purest statesman, of the first order of that unrivalled company of heroes, who founded our Republic.

Of John Jay, the Historian Hildreth remarks: "In lofty disinterestedness, in unyielding integrity, no one of the great men of the Revolution approached so near Washington."

We shall establish this position by the testimony of his contemporaries, and inasmuch as this great man was a thorough Reformed Episcopalian, and framed the original Protestant Episcopal Church upon the identical principles which characterize our Communion, we justly claim him as belonging to *us*. We fortunately, moreover, have his successive protests against the exclusive, sacerdotal, arrogant spirit which characterized the Protestant Episcopal Church, after the Constitution and Prayer Book which he, with his pre-eminent associates had constructed, was ignored; and a Communion based on opposite, anti-American, unsafe, and justly unpopular principles was substituted by the General Convention of 1789.

John Jay survived that Convention for thirty years. He foresaw the disastrous results which might occur through unwise legislation, and these, with his gifted co-laborers, he earnestly labored to preclude. His wise and faithful testimony may well be pondered by Protestant Episcopalians. Reformed Episcopalians will be strengthened and stimulated by its perusal.

We have lingered longer on the history of these departed Christian statesmen because they richly deserve to be recalled to our remembrance, who are enjoying the fruits of their sufferings, and their heroic struggles.

Their testimony to the soundness and substantial worth of our principles is conclusive and overwhelming, and inasmuch as in the contest for the liberties and rights of their country, they struggled and succeeded against almost insuperable difficulties, so may we, who inherit their ecclesiastical principles, finally triumph, in our stand for a primitive, Scriptural Episcopacy, and a pure, Protestant Liturgy.

HOW WASHINGTON REGARDED JAY.

When President Washington assumed his Office, he showed more confidence in John Jay than in any other of his contemporaries, for he offered him the choice of the offices within his gift. After Jay had been confirmed as Chief Justice, Washington writes : "In nominating you for the important station which you now fill, I only acted in conformity with my best judgment, but I trust did a grateful thing to the good citizens of these United States." Writings of Washington, X., 35.

THE OPINION OF JOHN ADAMS.

Similar was the opinion entertained of him by John Adams. "I often say that when my confidence in Mr. Jay shall cease, I must give up the cause of confidence and renounce it with all men," were the words of Adams; and when he appointed him Chief Justice, while Governor of New York, an office which he declined, he writes: "I had no permission from you to take this step, but it appeared to me that Providence has thrown in my way an opportunity not only of marking to the public the spot where, in my opinion, 'he greatest mass of worth remained collected in one individual, but of furnishing my country with the best security its inhabitants afforded against the increasing dissolution of morals." New York Review, Oct., 1841, p. 326. Letters of John Adams, Dec. 19, 1800.

EULOGIUM OF JOHN QUINCY ADAMS.

President John Quincy Adams in his Jubilee of the Constitution pronounced before the N. Y. Hist. Society, 1839, p. 96, thus succinctly sums up the character and services of this remarkable man: "Mr. Jay was then Chief Justice of the United States. And how shall I dare to speak to YOU of a native of your own State, and one of the brightest ornaments, not only of your State, but of his country and of human nature. At the dawn of manhood he had been one of the delegates from the *people* of New York, at the first Continental Congress of 1774. In the course of the Revolutionary War, he had been successively President of Congress, one of their ministers in Europe—one of the negotiators of the preliminary and definitive treaties of peace, and Secretary of Foreign Affairs to the Confederation Congress till the transition to the Constitutional government, and at the organization of the Judicial Tribunals of the Union was placed with the unanimous sanction of the public voice at their head. With this thickening crowd of honors gathering round him as he trod the path of life, he possessed with a perfectly self-controlled ambition, a fervently pious, meek and quiet, but firm and determined spirit. As one of the authors of the Federalist, and by official and personal influence as Secretary of Foreign Affairs, and as a most respected citizen of New York he had contributed essentially to the adoption of the Constitution."

Daniel Webster remarked, Wks., I., 207: " When the spotless ermine of the judicial robe fell on John Jay, it touched nothing less spotless than itself." " Go on, my friend," writes Robert Morris, " you deserve and will receive the gratitude of your Country. History will hand down your plaudits to posterity. The men of the present day, who are generally least grateful to their contemporaries, esteem it an honor to be of your acquaintance." Jay's Life, II., 110.

Gulian C. Verplanck thus eloquently expresses the general sentiment: "A halo of veneration seemed to encircle him as one belonging to another world, though lingering among us. When the tidings of his death came to us, they were received through the nation, not with sorrow or mourning, but with solemn awe, like that with which we read the mysterious passage of ancient Scripture, 'AND ENOCH WALKED WITH GOD, AND HE WAS NOT FOR GOD TOOK HIM.'" Vol. II., p. 463.

JAY A PROTESTANT CHURCHMAN.

It is not surprising that such an eminent Christian statesman should take a great interest in founding the future American Episcopal Church to which he was intelligently and devotedly attached.

Mr. Jay at that time, with James Duane was a Warden of Trinity Church, then as now the most prominent parish of its Communion. A descendant of the Huguenots he was a most unyielding Protestant. He was at the same time a thorough Episcopalian by inheritance and conviction.

INFLUENCE OF CONVERTS FROM PURITANISM.

There was this marked difference between the men who laid the original foundations of the Church in wisdom and moderation, and those through whom these foundations were overthrown.

At the time of the birth of Bishop Seabury, his father was a licensed Congregational preacher.

Bishop Parker was educated for the Congregational ministry. Bishop Bass, his predecessor in Massachusetts, preached four years as a Congregationalist.

The father of Bishop Jarvis renounced the Congregational Communion about the time of his son's birth.

Dr. Bela Hubbard was a Congregationalist at the time he graduated from college.

At the demand chiefly of these five clergymen, the grand American Episcopal work of Provoost, Jay and Duane; Griffith and Page; Pinckney and Peters, and their pre-eminent associates; old Episcopalians; was allowed to be dismantled, and the feudal product of the

Stewarts and the Non-Jurors, to be substituted in its room, and thus it has remained to the present day.

ECCLESIASTICAL CHANGES LEAD TO EXTREMES.

That the converts from the Puritan system became advocates of extreme Episcopal Liturgical views was natural, and the general extravagance of sentiment in these directions in the P. E. Communion, has its origin in that source, a change of base on the part of so many of its clergy. The late eminent Dr. Nott, wisely remarked: "Men who go over from one denomination to another always stand up more than straight, and for two reasons: First, to satisfy their new friends that they have heartily renounced their former error, and secondly, to convince their former friends that they had good reason for desertion."

The loyalty of Jay and Duane to their Church was unquestioned. The eminent Thomas Jones, a prominent loyalist and Church of England man, in his "History of New York," recently published, but written at the time of the Revolution, p. 35, writes: "Duane and Jay were both gentlemen of eminence in the law, had each a sufficiency of ambition, with a proper sense of pride, are both strong Episcopalians, and almost adored the British Constitution in Church and State."

EMINENT FITNESS OF JOHN JAY FOR THE WORK.

For the construction of the new Ecclesiastical Constitution and the preparation of the Liturgy and Offices, we see that Mr. Jay was fitted beyond most men; from his simple Scriptural piety, his pre-eminent experience as a statesman, his Christian studies, his singular moderation, and his almost unequalled gift as a writer. Of his memorable paper presented to Congress in 1774, on "The Rights of the Colonies in General," Mr. Jefferson said: "It is a production certainly of the finest pen in America."

In the Conventions of 1785 and 1786, the Constitution and Prayer Book were prepared. At the three Conventions either Mr. Jay or Duane were present, with Bishop Provoost. All were loyal Americans and liberal Churchmen, and concerted together to preserve the infant Communion free from the influence of the unsound and dangerous ecclesiastical principles, which were prominently represented by Bishop Seabury, who had been consecrated by the Scotch Non-Jurors in 1784.

As we shall show, these men were opposed to a union with Bishop Seabury, and purposely impressed principles upon the Constitution and Prayer Book, to which they were fully aware he was violently opposed. If these had been suffered to remain, the entangling and disastrous alliance would never have been consummated, and the Church would doubtless have been saved from its departure from its original principles; "Formed," as it was, in the words of this wise, Christian patriot, "after the Revolution, with an eye to what was then believed to be the truth and simplicity of the Gospel." Life of Jay, vol. I., p. 442.

When the General Convention assembled in Philadelphia in 1785, it was in pursuance of an invitation from a somewhat informal meeting in the city of New York, September, 1784, at which the leading spirits were of the Clergy, Rev. Messrs. White, Provoost, Wharton, Smith, and Griffith; and of the Laity, Messrs. Duane, Willett, Alsop, Willing, Peters and Powell. All of the Clergy here enumerated attended in 1785. Of the Laity, Willett, Alsop and Willing were absent. Their places were amply filled by other men of distinction, as Shippen, Hartley, Page and Pinckney.

DANGERS TO BE AVOIDED.

In framing the Constitution, there was especial need to guard against the claim of exclusive Divine right on the part of the Episcopate, priestly functions on the part of the presbyters, and the denial of the co-ordinate rights of the laity.

These claims had been asserted in the State of Connecticut, where the clergy in secret council, without lay co-operation, which was carefully ignored, had chosen one for Bishop who had been consecrated under peculiar circumstances, such as had created alarm among the patriotic Episcopalians of New York, Virginia, and South Carolina.

It will be seen that men like Provoost, Duane, Page and Pinckney, who had suffered in establishing the Republic, took good care that the rights of the laity should be protected, and that the claims and prerogatives of the Bishops, an order through whose agency, the Puritans had been compelled to leave their native country; who had legislated as spiritual lords in England, and through whose influence the non-conformist clergy had been brutally ejected; should be relegated to their position in the Primitive Church, simply that of Presiding Presbyters, chosen by the voice of the people.

THE POSITION OF BISHOPS.

Therefore, in framing the Constitution, these intelligent Christian legislators inserted as the third Article, the following: "In every State where there shall be a bishop duly consecrated and settled, and who shall have acceeded to this General Ecclesiastical Constitution, he shall be considered as a member of the Convention *ex officio*.

It was the design to prevent in the future Church the dangerous aggrandizement of power by the Bishops, in constituting a separate House, and that this was the settled purpose of these legislators is more clearly evident from the action at the next Convention in 1786, when on the motion of Dr. White, this section was thus amended: "In every State where there shall be a bishop duly consecrated and settled, and who shall have acceded to the Articles of this Ecclesiastical Constitution, he shall be considered as a member of the General Convention *ex officio*; and a bishop shall always preside in the General Convention, if any of the Episcopal order be present."

NO SEPARATE HOUSE OF BISHOPS.

It is evident how carefully these clear-headed patriots guarded against the evil of allowing the bishops to legislate as a separate order, and thus secure to the clergy an overwhelming preponderance of power.

The Convention had carefully protected the rights of the clerical order by adopting the principle set forth in the preliminary meeting of 1784, as follows: "That the Clergy and Laity assembled in Convention, shall deliberate in one body, but shall vote separately; and the concurrence of both shall be necessary to give validity to every measure."

Thus, two principles were clearly established. That there should not be two separate Houses to legislate; and moreover that Clergy and Laity should have co-ordinate powers. This was the Rational, Republican, and Primitive System adopted by the Revolutionary Episcopalians.

And that this was deliberately done, with admirable forethought, becomes more evident from the action of Duane and Jay, evidently with the concurrence of Bishop Provoost, when these distinguished statesmen were both Wardens of Trinity Church, and Bishop Provoost was Rector.

MR. JAY'S RESOLUTION FOR PROTECTION OF THE LAITY.

In the meeting of the Vestry, October, 1789, to appoint delegates to the General Convention of that year, Mr. Jay moved that the Corporation would adopt the following resolution, viz.: "That the delegates now chosen to represent this congregation at the next Convention be, and they hereby are, instructed not to consent to, but on the contrary, to oppose every proposed Constitution for the American Episcopal Church, and every proposed alteration in the one of 1786, that shall not give to the laity equal powers with the clergy in the making of all acts, laws, and regulations binding on the Church."

The patriotic vestry of 1784 having been removed, and a new one from the old loyalist element who had returned to the city, having been chosen, the wardens were overborne, and the consideration of the resolution postponed. Berrian's Hist. of Trinity Church, p. 176.

Jay and Duane sought by this vigorous resolution to forestall the efforts of the party who desired to unite with Bishop Seabury and the New England Loyalists, who demanded as a condition of union, that the Bishops should legislate as a separate order, with the veto power on the Lower House, thus giving to the clergy a duplicated power over the laity, through the votes of two distinct clerical orders.

THE PATRIOT CHURCHMEN DEFEATED.

How Seabury and his party triumphed, and how the feudal system was stamped upon the Protestant Episcopal Church by the abandonment of the Constitution framed by the eminent statesmen of the Revolution, will be narrated in its proper place.

ANOTHER DANGER.

These wise statesmen of 1785 sought to guard against another danger. The Church of England in New York, Connecticut and New Jersey, had been mostly loyal to the Crown.

To the southward its members had more generally espoused the Cause of Liberty, Justice and the Revolution. We have previously shown how that if the Cause of Liberty and Independence had rested with Episcopalians alone, it would have failed.

The Convention of 1785 determined to secure to the infant Church a patriotic clergy, who would be in sympathy with the new Republic, and would be therefore fitted to be instructors of the rising generation, in the patriotic, American principles of its noble founders.

SERVICE FOR THE FOURTH OF JULY.

Fresh from service and suffering in the State, and in the field, they thus ordered: "On motion, Resolved, That the Fourth of July shall be observed by this Church for ever, as a day of Thanksgiving to Almighty God, for the inestimable blessings of religious and civil liberty vouchsafed to the United States of America."

"The Rev. Dr. Smith, from the committee to prepare a form of prayer and thanksgiving for the Fourth of July, reported that they had prepared the same. Ordered, That it now be received and read. Ordered, That the said report be received and read by paragraphs; which being done, Resolved, That the said form of prayer be used in this Church, on the Fourth of July for ever."

Thus was the Church consecrated to free, American principles, by this careful, deliberate action.

SOUTH CAROLINA AND PENNSYLVANIA RESOLUTIONS.

And with respect to this Fourth of July service which is one admirably constructed and eminently suitable, we find that the Convention of South Carolina of 1786, reaffirmed a resolution passed by the P. E. Convention of Pennsylvania, viz: "That the Fourth of July shall be observed by this Church forever as a day of thanksgiving to Almighty God, for the inestimable blessings of religious and civil liberty vouchsafed to the United States of America." In Charleston, religious services on that day were attended by great numbers of rejoicing worshipers. The large churches of St. Philip's and St. Michael's were crowded with attendants. Is it wonderful that when those patriots, with those of Virginia heard that at the Convention of 1789, through the influence of the Loyalists of New York and New England, the Fourth of July service had been rejected and eliminated, and that the Non-Juring principles had triumphed in the overthrow of the Scripturally revised Book of Common Prayer, that the Church at the South received a fatal blow from which it has never fully recovered?

OPINION OF JOHN ADAMS.

These Southern patriots whose lands had suffered so grievously in the war that had achieved American Independence, felt justly with John Adams, as he wrote to his wife on the 5th of July, 1776: "The Fourth of July, 1776, will be a memorable epoch in the history of America. I am apt to believe it will be celebrated by succeeding generations as the great anniversary festival. It ought to be commemorated as the day of deliverance, by solemn acts of devotion to Almighty God. It ought to be solemnized with pomps, shows, games, sports, guns, bells, bon-fires and illuminations, from one end of the continent to the other, from this time forward forever."

The Protestant Episcopal Church did not fail in its duty of commemorating this grandest of political events; it was only when it was handed over to those who had sought to keep the nation in the hands of its tyrants, that the celebration which so emphatically condemned their previous history was disallowed, and thereby the confidence of the nation justly and irreparably forfeited.

BISHOP WHITE'S DEFENSE UNTENABLE.

The very reasoning by which Bishop White would palliate his unjustifiable assent to the destruction of this wise and fitting work of his patriotic fellow-laborers of 1785 and 1786, carries its own condemnation. He writes, Mem. p. 105: "Greater stress is laid on this matter, because of the notorious fact, that the majority of the clergy could not have used the service without subjecting themselves to ridicule and censure." But what did the American people want with religious teachers who did not accept heartily the principles of the Declaration of Independence? Were they fitted to be instructors of the rising generation? Would not the infant Church have been better served by fewer ministers, but who were in sympathy with the masses of the victorious and triumphant nation, fresh from the sufferings endured in the great struggle? But, as we have before remarked, this insane passion for uniformity, and for an aggregation of utterly uncongenial elements was then, as it has been since, the bane of the Protestant Episcopal Church. The action of the Convention of 1789 utterly destroyed all prospect of that Church becoming, what it might have been, and was entitled to be, among the largest, most acceptable and most influential of American Churches. As a legitimate and necessary result it has sunk numerically to the third class and ranks as seventh.

Bishop Provoost writes in 1786: "The thanksgiving for the Fourth of July in all probability, is one principal cause of the opposition to the alterations in the Book."

Most unfortunately the opposition of Seabury and his friends prevailed. "Peace at any price," was to be secured, even by a discreditable and disastrous change of base.

The public enemies of the Revolution were admitted to a predominating influence, and with their admission the Constitution and Liturgy of Jay, Duane, Page, Pinckney, Griffin and Peters, was sacrificed on the altar of a false and hollow union.

THE RADICAL CHANGE IN THE CONSTITUTION.

We have seen how carefully the framers of the Constitution of 1785, avoided the evils which had attended the Church in its past experience, from the principle of Divine Right, in a third Order of Ministers, to whom had been committed the exclusive power of Ordination, Confirmation, and Jurisdiction. They gave to the Laity a co-ordinate power of Legislation, and reducing the Episcopate to its original Scriptural arrangement, an order identical with the Presbyterate, they constituted the General Convention with but one House for the transaction of Ecclesiastial work.

At the next Convention of 1786, they affirmed the Primitive principle, that the Bishop should be "primus inter pares," and ordered that "a Bishop shall always preside in the General Convention, if any of the Episcopal order be present." Thus the Constitution remained until the year 1789. Drs. Provoost and White in the mean time had been consecrated Bishops.

HOW THE CHANGE WAS EFFECTED.

But, as we have seen, there was another Bishop who had been consecrated under very different circumstances. Elected secretly by ten Presbyters, without the knowledge or concurrence of the Laity, refused consecration by the Bishops of the Church of England, Dr. Seabury had been consecrated by the Non-Juring Bishops of Scotland, whose views of doctrine and discipline were not in accord with the framers of the Constitution and Prayer Book of 1785.

The Preface of the Prayer Book of 1785 states plainly that the principles of the Divines who were loyal to William III. and the amendments proposed by those eminent Reformers, had been incorporated in the primary, American, Episcopal Liturgy.

Recognizing no Church not Episcopal, Bishop Seabury and the New England clergy, were entirely cut off from fraternal ecclesiastical relations with any ecclesiastical body, unless a union was formed with that represented by Bishops Provoost and White.

This union was earnestly desired. But the understanding upon which Bishop Seabury received consecration, was that Laymen were not to legislate for the Church, and moreover that the distinct assent of Bishops as a superior order by Divine right was essential to the validity of Ecclesiastical proceedure.

The Constitution and Prayer Book of 1785 were framed in accordance with the principles of the glorious Revolution of William III. which were in consonance with those of the American Revolution.

But the principles of Bishop Seabury and his friends were avowedly the same as those of the Bishops of James II. and these same divines had been outspoken opponents of the patriots who had secured liberty to the American Colonies. They had written, and preached, and prayed, and labored, in the cause of the invading armies.

BISHOP WHITE YIELDS THE MAIN PRINCIPLE.

Lamentable and strange is the fact that Bishop White yielded the main points in the controversy; allowed the Constitution and Prayer Book of 1785 to be overthrown; and although Laymen were admitted to legislate in Conventions, yet the readmission of the priestly principle of the ministry, and the adoption of a separate House of Bishops, with an absolute negative on the acts of the lower House, destroyed the safeguards erected by the Revolutionary Fathers, and prepared the way for errors and disasters which have naturally followed such a weak, unwise, inconsistent, and indefensible surrender of the principles adopted and affirmed by the great and good men who founded the American Protestant Episcopal Church.

In 1789 this radical and revolutionary change was made in the constitution framed in 1785.

Article III. of the Constitution of 1789 reads thus:

"The Bishops of this Church, when there shall be three or more, shall, whenever General Conventions are held, form a separate House, with a right to originate and propose acts, for the concurrence of the House of Deputies, composed of Clergy and Laity; and when any proposed act shall have passed the House of Deputies, the same shall be transmitted to the House of Bishops, who shall have a negative thereupon, unless adhered to by four fifths of the other House; and all acts of the Convention shall be authenticated by both Houses."

THE CONVENTION OF 1808.

In the later General Convention of 1808, the words: "unless adhered to by four fifths of the lower House" was struck out, and thus an absolute veto was given to the House of Bishops upon the proceedings of the entire body of Presbyters and Laymen of the lower House. The feudal system was thus permanently engrafted upon the Protestant Episcopal Church. The sad results which have attended its later history are the simple, logical outcome upon such retrogressive and humiliating legislation.

It is very remarkable that when this complete

surrender to the principle of exclusive Episcopal Divine right was made; Bishops White and Claggett alone composed the upper House, and thus it was in the power of Bishop White to have prevented this utter overthrow of a vital, cardinal principle of the Constitution of 1785, which he had assisted in drafting.

In the Convention of 1789, Bishops White and Seabury were the sole members of the House of Bishops, when the first serious abandonment of the essential principles of the primary Constitution occurred, and thus again, we are sorry to say, is Bishop White to be held responsible for the disastrous changes which were then effected.

THE DECLINE OF THE CHURCH.

So greatly had the Church declined after the unhappy legislation of 1789, that in the Convention of 1808, when the fundamental change was effected which threw the Church into the power of the Bishops, there were present but fourteen clergymen and thirteen laymen, with scarce a man of eminence among them; in sad contrast to that remarkable and more numerous body of Christian patriots and divines, who framed that admirable Constitution, and that Protestant Prayer Book, upon which the Reformed Episcopal Church has, under Divine Providence, happily re-erected and restored the Church of the Fathers.

THE INFLUENCE OF BISHOPS SEABURY AND HOBART.

Dr. Hobart, afterwards consecrated Bishop in 1811, was the most able, influential, and energetic member of that small Convention, which surrendered the principle of co-ordinate lay legislation to the feudal principle of exclusive Divine right of the Episcopal Order. This sound and salutary safeguard of the rights of the people, affirmed and re-affirmed in three Conventions by Dr. White as a Presbyter, in co-operation with the Christian statesmen of the Revolution, was abandoned by Bishop White under the influence of the stronger will and more vigorous and energetic nature of Seabury and Hobart, both honest and uncompromising High Churchmen. These two prelates succeeded in overthrowing the work of the Revolutionary pioneers of the Church, constituted essentially a new Church, and thus compelled, in less than a century, a return to the original principles of their Communion, of those Episcopalians who desired to worship God, with a pure Scriptural Liturgy, and by a discipline in consonance with the Church in the days of the Apostles. The Reformed Episcopal Church is not a new sect, but the old Church revived. Its history is closely analogous to that of the parent Church of England, which at the time of the Reformation, preserved its Episcopal Order, and simply returned to the primitive doctrines held, when Christianity was first planted in the Apostolic era, in Great Britain.

REVISIONS OF THE PRAYER BOOK, PROTESTANT AND OTHERWISE.

There have been *eight* prominent revisions of the Book of Common Prayer; four in the interest of Tradition, Ritualism, and Low Popery or Semi-Romanism; four based on Holy Scripture, Spiritual Christianity, and Protestantism.

The first *four*: the Revision of Elizabeth, 1559; of James I, 1604; of Charles II, 1662; of Bishop Seabury, 1789; which last is the present Book of the Protestant Episcopal Church.

The other *four*: the Revision of Edward VI, 1552; of William III, 1689; of Bishop White and the Revolutionary statesmen, 1785; of Bishop Cummins, 1874; which is the Prayer Book of the Reformed Episcopal Church.

This last Revision has had a longer life than all the other Protestant revisions combined. The Reform has been radical, consistent, and complete, and the Book has come to stay.

THE REVISIONS OF 1874 AND 1785 IDENTICAL IN PRINCIPLE.

We propose to show briefly that the Book of 1874 is identical in principle with that of 1785, and is irreconcilable with that of 1789, which contains the false doctrines of the Revision of 1662.

THE OMISSION OF THE TERM "PRIEST."

First: like the Book of 1785, that of 1874 has eliminated entirely from its pages the word *priest* as applied to a human minister; in the Prayer Books of 1552 and of 1559, the clergy are designated by the term minister.

The term "priest" was substituted for minister in the revision of Charles II, 1662.

It was removed by our Revolutionary Fathers in the Book of 1785. It is not introduced in the Reformed Episcopal Book of 1874.

Through the influence of Bishop Seabury it was re-inserted in the Book of 1789, and fifteen years later an Institution Service was added, containing the terms "Altar," "Sacerdotal function," Sacerdotal connexion," "Sacerdotal relation." Thus the so-called "*Protestant* Episcopal Prayer Book" has been made the most priestly, sacerdotal, and sacramental Liturgy framed since the Reformation. The Ritualism which has abounded, is the simple, natural, logical outcome of the phraseology contained in the Book. Its advocates hold the fort and can not be dislodged.

SIMILARITY OF BAPTISMAL SERVICES.

Secondly: *The Baptismal Services* of the Books of 1785 and of 1874 are in irreconciliable antagonism to those of 1662 and 1789. In the Book of 1785, as in that of 1874, the declaration "Seeing now, dearly beloved brethren, that this child is regenerated, &c.," is entirely omitted.

In the Book of 1785, after the Baptism, instead of the words of the Book of 1789, "We yield Thee hearty thanks, most merciful Father, that it has pleased Thee to regenerate this infant with the Holy Spirit, &c.," we have this prayer: "We yield Thee hearty thanks, most merciful Father, that it has pleased Thee to receive this infant as Thine own child by Baptism, and to incorporate him into Thy Holy Church.

In the Book of 1874, the language is: "We yield Thee humble thanks, O Heavenly Father, that Thou hast inclined us to dedicate this child to Thee in Baptism; and we humbly pray that Thy grace may enable us to bring him up in the nurture and admonition of the Lord, &c."

In the Book of 1785, the Catechism and Confirmation Service were likewise essentially modified, and made to conform in doctrine to the other Scriptural alterations.

We give the main points of difference between the Books of 1785 and 1874, which abjure the doctrine of Baptismal Regeneration; and those of 1789 and 1662, which affirm that error unmistakably and designedly.

The two former Books have affirmed the Protestant and Scriptural Doctrine of Baptism; the two latter have retained the teaching of the Roman Catholic Liturgies. This is another cause of the extensive growth of anti-Protestant error in the Protestant Episcopal Church.

AS TO THE LORD'S SUPPER.

Thirdly: With respect to the Lord's Supper. There is an important doctrinal difference between the Books of 1785 and 1874, together with that of 1662; as compared with the Protestant Episcopal Book of 1789.

In the three former are omitted what is styled the form of Oblation of the elements of Bread and Wine, which is contained in the Scottish Communion Service.

Bishop Seabury, as we shall show more fully hereafter, held to the doctrine that the Offering of our Lord Jesus Christ for the salvation of mankind, was made especially at the time He instituted the Lord's Supper, rather than on the Cross, and therefore he insisted that the language of the Scotch Communion Service, which may be thus interpreted, should be introduced into the Prayer Book of 1789. This "Invocation" and "Oblation," were purposely omitted in the Books of 1785 and 1874. As they are not contained in the English Book of 1662, the American Protestant Episcopal Prayer Book favors the Romish doctrine of the Lord's Supper more strongly than the former. So essential did Bishop Seabury regard these words in the office for Holy Communion, that, according to Bishop White, he refused to lead in the celebration of the Lord's Supper at the General Convention, when they were not used. Not only is the "Oblation," and the "Invocation" by the "Priest" omitted in the Book of 1874, but there is appended this important Rubric: "In conducting this service, except when kneeling, the minister shall face the people."

Moreover, another Rubric similar to that of the Book of 1662 is added: " The Act and Prayer of Consecration do not change the nature of the elements, but merely set them apart for a holy use; and the reception of them in a kneeling posture is not an act of adoration of the elements."

The Communion Service of the Book of 1789 is not thus guarded.

The IX. Article of the R. E. Constitution reads:

"Nothing calculated to teach—either directly or symbolically—that the Christian Ministry possesses a Sacerdotal character, or that the Lord's Supper is a Sacrifice, shall ever be allowed in the Worship of this Church; nor shall any Communion Table be constructed in the form of an altar."

In the Reformed Episcopal Book every avenue to Romanism has been carefully closed.

CHANGES IN THE ORDINAL.

Fourthly: *In the Forms of Ordination.* Here is a marked and radical difference between the Books of 1789 and 1874.

There being no Bishops to confer orders, the preparation of such forms was deferred by the members of the Conventions of 1785 and 1786. The doctrine was then established that there were no human Priests, nor a third order of ministers by Divine right.

In the Prayer Book of 1789, the Primitive, Protestant and Scriptural principles were abandoned, and Consecration and Ordination Offices prepared according to the Non-Juring doctrines of Bishop Seabury, which were similar to those of Archbishop Laud.

The *Offices* for the *Consecration* of *Bishops* and *Ordination* of *Priests* in the Book of 1789, were framed on the model of the Book of 1662. This later Revision differed from the Reformers' Book of 1552, in that it made Episcopal Consecration and Ordination essential to the ministry, for the first time in the history of the Church of England. Though Bishop White and his co-laborers of 1785 did not hold this doctrine, it was inserted to reconcile Bishop Seabury and the Clergy of exclusive and Sacerdotal views. The term "Priest" was borrowed from the Book of 1662, a term which had been carefully excluded from the Revision of 1552, and from all later Revisions for over a century.

This same term of Priest, together with the notion of exclusive, Episcopal, Divine right, as we have seen, was expunged by the Revolutionary Revisers of 1785, as it was by Bishop Cummins, and the framers of the Book of 1874.

In the Ordinal for Priests in the Protestant Episcopal Prayer Book, the form is this: "Receive the Holy Ghost for the Office and Work of a Priest in the

Church of God, now committed unto thee by the Imposition of our hands. Whose sins thou dost forgive, they are forgiven; and whose sins thou dost retain, they are retained. And be thou a faithful Dispenser of the Word of God and of His Holy Sacraments, etc."

THE PROTESTANT EPISCOPAL FORM DERIVED FROM THE MIDDLE AGES.

If this language means anything, it is that the absolution of sins is the primal work of the Protestant Episcopal Priest, and those who act on this principle are acting according to the Record. Inasmuch as this form was not in use till the Middle Ages, in the thirteenth century, it is not wonderful that the doctrines of that superstitious period, connected with a human priesthood, a material altar, and a memorial sacrifice, have largely leavened the Protestant Episcopal Church.

In the Prayer Book of 1874, the form of Ordination reads: "Take thou Authority to execute the office of a Presbyter in the Church of God, now committed unto thee; and be thou a faithful Dispenser of the Word of God and of His Holy Ordinances, etc."

In the Book of 1789 are clearly contained the doctrines of an exclusive Episcopal Ordination; of Priestly functions; of tactual Succession; and of transmitted grace. In the Book of 1874, these errors are expressly and repeatedly denied.

DECLARATION OF PRINCIPLES.

In her Statement of Principles, the Reformed Episcopal Church declares: "This Church recognizes and adheres to Episcopacy, not as of Divine right, but as a very ancient and desirable form of Church polity."

She "condemns and rejects the following erroneous and strange doctrines as contrary to God's Word:

"*First*, That the Church of Christ exists only in one order or form of Ecclesiastical polity;

"*Second*, That Christian ministers are 'priests' in another than that in which all believers are a 'royal priesthood;'

"*Third*, That the Lord's Table is an altar on which the oblation of the Body and Blood of Christ is offered anew to the Father;

"*Fourth*, That the presence of Christ in the Lord's

Supper is a presence in the elements of the Bread and Wine;

"*Fifth*, That Regeneration is inseparably connected with Baptism."

THE TWENTY-FOURTH ARTICLE.

And still further to emphasize her rejection of these Mediæval errors which have so sadly corrupted the Church, she declares in her XXIV. Article: "That doctrine of 'Apostolic Succession,' by which it is taught that the ministry of the Christian Church must be derived through a series of uninterrupted ordinations, whether by tactual succession or otherwise, and that without the same there can be no valid ministry, no Christian Church, and no due ministration of Baptism and the Lord's Supper, is wholly rejected as unscriptural, and productive of great mischief.

This Church values its historic ministry, but recognizes and honors as equally valid, the ministry of other Churches, even as God the Holy Ghost has accompanied their work with demonstration and power."

Moreover, by the R. E. Canons it is ordered, that a Presbyter from another Church may be received without reordination; pulpit exchanges with ministers of Evangelical Churches are allowed; letters dismissory are given to Bishops and Presbyters desiring to change their ecclesiastical relations; and parishes may be formed without the consent of neighboring pastors and congregations.

In the Protestant Episcopal Church, on the other hand, reordination is required of all adhering non-Episcopal ministers, while Roman Priests are admitted without it; the pulpit is barred to all without Episcopal orders; all who leave its ministry for other Churches are deposed; and the assent of a majority of neighboring rectors is required, before a new parish can be formed.

So thoroughly antagonistic are the two Churches in their principles and practices.

THE MISSION OF THE REFORMED EPISCOPAL CHURCH.

Thus has the Reformed Episcopal Church been loyal to the Truth of Holy Scripture, and to the doctrine and practice of the Primitive Church.

Thus does she stand on the foundation of the martyrs

of Edward VI.; of the Reformers under William III.; of the Revolutionary Founders of American Episcopacy.

In Divine Providence, to this Church has been committed the noble and necessary work of restoring in this age, the principles from which the Protestant Episcopal Church, in 1789, radically diverged; a divergence which for near a century has grown wider and wider; and has compelled at last the sacrifices and toils, by which, through the manly courage and enlightened faith of Bishop Cummins and his co-laborers, the grand and holy work has been successfully and permanently inaugurated.

CAUSES OF THE OPPOSITION TO BISHOP SEABURY.

It has been shown that the overthrow of the Primary Constitution and Prayer Book of the Divines and Statesmen of the Revolution, framed in 1785 and 1786, was due mainly to Bishop Seabury, of Connecticut.

The strong opposition to this Prelate manifested by Bishop Provoost, John Jay, James Duane, and others at that period, has been alluded to.

We propose to give the reasons why these eminent Episcopalians of the Revolutionary period endeavored to prevent an ecclesiastical union with this energetic, non-juring Bishop.

BISHOP PROVOOST ASSAILED FOR HIS OPPOSITION.

This opposition was very plainly expressed. Bishop Provoost has been severely handled in the "Church Review," and by various writers, for the part he took in the matter. Referring to a correspondence of the distinguished Granville Sharp with Dr. Manning, an eminent Baptist, and Bishop Provoost, with respect to the non-recognition of Bishop Seabury's Consecration, this "Review" remarks: " It was the old scene at Jerusalem re-enacted, Herod and Pilate—the determined dissenter and the jealous Churchman—were made friends in their common antipathy to one both innocent and unsuspecting." Bishop Provoost is charged with being " unkind," " discourteous," " bitter," " implacable," " malicious," " a troubler in Israel," " low in morals and belief," on account of his manly, conscientious effort to preserve the infant, Protestant Episcopal Church from the dangerous, semi-Romish, and anti-Republican principles of the able and adroit leader of the Tory clergy of the Revolution. See Am. Quar. Church Review for July, 1862, April 1863. The *International Review*, April, 1881, p. 324, states: "Bishop W. S. Perry, of Iowa, the laborious, and probably in the view of some of his Communion, the disagreeably candid historian of the Colonial Church, has put into print a pamphlet containing such a severe judgment of the first Bishop of New York as to leave his readers to infer that Provoost's ' consecration ' did not reach to his character." Beardsley's History of the P. E. Church in Connecticut, contains the usual High Church depreciation of this accomplished and patriotic friend and pastor of Jay, Duane, the Livingstons, Hamilton, Rufus King, and other great statesmen of the Revolution.

VINDICATION OF BISHOP PROVOOST.

The succeeding history of the P. E. Church furnishes ample justification for the warnings, and precautionary measures of Bishop Provoost.

Of his exalted character and services, in addition to the full and varied testimony we have previously presented, there is ample vindication in the resolutions passed by the Convention of his Diocese in this language: " Justly reposing the highest confidence in your integrity and piety, your love of peace and order, and your unremitted endeavors for the advancement of true religion and virtue, we rejoice that the distinguished honor of filling one of the first Episcopal Chairs in these United States hath been conferred on a character so truly amiable, and we trust that we, and those whom we represent, shall never fail to render you all due support, respect and reverence * * * an example for our imitation, and an ornament to our holy religion." See Berrian's Hist. of Trinity Church, p. 207.

Well would it be for the defamers of this departed Christian Bishop if they might hand down to their posterity such a testimonial from such a constituency.

As Bishop Provoost opposed the election of Dr. Hobart to the Episcopate on much the same grounds as he did union with Bishop Seabury, much of the abuse he has received can be readily accounted for.

PLAIN LANGUAGE OF BISHOP PROVOOST.

Bishop Provoost saw the impending peril, and labored earnestly to prevent the catastrophe. He writes to

Bishop White, after the Convention of 1785, with reference to the applications for Episcopal Consecration: "I expect no obstruction to our application but what may arise from the intrigues of the Non-Juring Bishop of Connecticut, who a few days since paid a visit to this State, notwithstanding he incurred the guilt of misprision of treason, and was liable to confinement for life for doing so * * *. While he was there, a piece appeared in a paper under Rivington's direction, pretending to give an account of the late Convention, but replete with falsehood and prevarication, and evidently intended to create a prejudice against our transactions both in England and America." Later he writes: "If we may judge from appearances, Dr. Cebra and his friends are using every art to prevent the success of our application to the English prelates." The next year Bishop Provoost writes: "As the General Convention did not think proper to acknowledge Dr. Cebra as a Bishop, much less as a Bishop of our Church, it would be highly improper for us, in our private capacities, to give any sanction to his Ordinations. It would also be an insult upon the Church and the truly venerable prelates to whom we are now making application for the Succession. For my own part, I carry the matter still further, and as a friend to the liberties of mankind, should be extremely sorry that the conduct of my brethren here should tend to the resurrection of the sect of Non-Jurors (nearly buried in oblivion), whose slavish and absurd tenets were a disgrace to humanity, and God grant that they may never be cherished in America, which, as my native Country, I wish may always be sacred to Liberty, both civil and religious." February 24th, 1789, Bishop Provoost writes thus plainly to Bishop Seabury: "An invitation to the Church in that State (Connecticut) to meet us in General Convention, I conceive to be neither necessary nor proper; not necessary because I am informed that they have already appointed two persons to attend the next General Convention without our invitation; nor proper because it is so publicly known that they have adopted a form of Church government which renders them inadmissible as members of the Convention or union." "Cebra" is stated to be one of the forms of the family name. A resolution offered by Bishop Provoost in the Convention of 1785, and passed, was as follows: "That the persons appointed to represent this Church be instructed not to consent to any acts that may imply the validity of Dr. Seabury's ordinations."

ACTIVE OPPOSITION OF JAY AND DUANE.

The opposition of John Jay and James Duane to the views of Bishop Seabury, and to ecclesiastical connection with him, was equally determined and well known. When the General Convention of 1789 was about to meet, while Jay and Duane were wardens of Trinity Church, New York, the former introduced, at a meeting of the Vestry, a resolution instructing the deputies to General Convention to oppose every alteration in the Constitution of 1785, which denied to the laity a co-ordinate power of legislation with the clergy.

When the General Convention had surrendered to Bishop Seabury and his friends, and a motion was made to agree to the new feudal Constitution, Jay and Duane voted to reject it, together with Mr. Farquhar, another distinguished patriot, and Anthony L. Bleecker.

The Vestry being now mainly composed of the returned opponents of the Revolution, the resolution was carried, and these wise and eminent patriots failed in their efforts to save the Church of their ancestors.

John Jay was an intelligent and consistent opponent of the principles of Bishop Seabury and of Bishop Hobart to the day of his death. Thirty years after his earnest efforts to preserve his Church from the blundering and pernicious legislation by which its hold upon the confidence and support of the American people was so sadly and needlessly lost, he wrote a letter to the corporation of Trinity Church, of which he had been the most illustrious member in an era of great men.

JAY ON APOSTOLIC SUCCESSION.

He is presenting his reason why the Institution Service would not be allowed in the parish. After showing its "unconstitutional assumptions of power, an insuperable objection," he proceeds to condemn the term "ministers of Apostolic Succession," as therein contained. He remarks: "If it be asked, whether the ministers of the Calvinistic and other Churches are of Apostolic Succession, it is answered by all our bishops and clergy that they are not. It follows, therefore, of necessary consequence, that our bishops and clergy and their congregation, when they offer up their prayer to Almighty God, must offer it with the meaning and understanding that the gracious promise mentioned in it is confined to Episcopalian ministers, and therefore excludes the ministers of all other denominations of Christians."

It is a marked coincidence, that this extreme Sacerdotal Institution Service was framed by a divine who had received his principles and his orders, like Bishop Seabury, from the Non-Juring Bishops of Scotland. Thus another sad legacy has descended from the same fountain of ecclesiastical bigotry and error to corrupt and distract the Church.

Referring to the divine blessings which had for centuries been distributed so copiously to Churches not Episcopalian, Mr. Jay most sagely writes: "It may not be unworthy of remark, that as a prophecy is best understood from its completion, so the manner in which a Divine promise is performed, affords the best exhibition of its true and original meaning." He alludes to our Saviour's words: "Lo, I am with you alway, even unto the end of the world;" which are restricted in their meaning by Roman Catholics and many Episcopalians, to their respective denominations.

We cannot refrain from quoting from the concluding words of this memorable letter of this pre-eminent Christian statesman, whose views were identical with those taught by the Reformed Episcopal Church. They are like a legacy from one of the old prophets.

A MEMORABLE INDICTMENT OF HIGH CHURCH EPISCOPACY.

"For a considerable time past we have observed a variety of circumstances connected with Church affairs which, on being combined and compared one with the other, justify inferences which, in our opinion, are exceedingly interesting, not only to the rights of the laity, but also to our churches in general, and to yours in particular. We allude to the gradual introduction and industrious propagation of High Church doctrines. Of late years, they have frequently been seen lifting up their heads and appearing in places where their presence was neither necessary nor expected. There never was a time when those doctrines promoted peace on earth or good will among men. Originating under the auspices and in the days of darkness and despotism, they patronized darkness and despotism, down to the Reformation. Ever encroaching on the rights of governments and people, they have constantly found it convenient to incorporate as far as possible, the claims of the clergy with the principles and practice of religion ; and their advocates have not ceased to preach for Christian doctrines, the commandments of men.

"To you it cannot be necessary to observe, that High Church doctrines are not accommodated to the state of society, nor to the tolerant principles, nor to the ardent love of liberty which prevail in our country. It is well known that our Church was formed after the Revolution, with an eye to what was then believed to be the truth and simplicity of the Gospel; and there appears to be some reason to regret that the motives which then governed have since been less operative * * * *.

"Whatever may be the result, we shall have the satisfaction of reflecting that we have done our duty, in thus explicitly protesting against measures and proceedings which, if persevered in, must and will, sooner or later, materially affect the tranquility and welfare of the Church." Jay's Life, vol. 1, p. 439-42.

Mr. Jay believed in Episcopacy in the primitive simplicity and purity which he had vainly sought to impress permanently upon his Church in its early American history.

He writes, p. 435: "We believe that Episcopacy was of Apostolic institution, but we do not believe in the various High Church doctrines and prerogatives which art and ambition, triumphing over credulity and weakness, have annexed to it."

MR. JAY AN ANTAGONIST OF BISHOP HOBART.

With such principles we are not surprised that Mr. Jay vigorously opposed the views and measures of Bishop Seabury, as he did for thirty years those of Bishop Hobart, who held to equally extreme and dangerous notions of Episcopal power and prerogative.

Thus, when Bishop Hobart assailed the American Bible Society, inasmuch as he disapproved of Episcopalians uniting with Christians of other names in extending the Gospel; Mr. Jay, as the foremost champion of enlightened and tolerant Protestant Episcopacy, repeatedly accepted the Presidency of the same Society, and vindicated it in his addresses against the assaults of its bigoted adversaries. Unfortunately the warnings of this Christian Patriarch were unheeded.

A SIMILAR REBUKE FROM THE SON OF JOHN JAY.

That his fears were realized, is seen in the letter of his distinguished son, Hon. William Jay, written to the rector of Trinity Church, a generation later, in 1856. He says in his published letter, p. 12: "To those who embrace the *Church principles* of Trinity, the very term Protestant is an offense. * * * * You know the lamentations which have been uttered over our uncatholic designation. The 'sound Church principles' which you tell us have at 'all times' been manfully maintained by Trinity, have in latter years brought forth their legitimate fruit, now known as Puseyism. This fruit has indeed wrought sore maladies, wild hallucinations, and wondrous mutations, in those who have partaken of it.

"It has metamorphosed one of our rectors into a Popish Bishop, and one of our Bishops into a *lay* Professor of a Jesuit college. It has driven the son of another Bishop from the ministry of the Church, and sent him an apostate on a pilgrimage to the Roman Pontiff, and—but I forbear. It is needless to dwell on the distractions, the heart-burnings, the mummeries, the puerilities, the symbolisms, and the awful apostacies resulting from the taste of this baneful and intoxicating fruit."

THE CHURCH'S RETURN TO PRIMITIVE PURITY OF DOCTRINE.

The evil leaven introduced into the Prayer Book and Constitution of 1789, blossomed and fruited, until its direful results within a century, compelled the return to the original principles of the Fathers; and with the blessing of God, was followed, through the agency of Bishop Cummins, by the free, enlightened Constitution, and the Protestant, Scriptural and Primitive Prayer Book of 1874 of the Reformed Episcopal Church.

THE ERRONEOUS DOCTRINES OF BISHOP SEABURY.

We desire it to be understood, that in our examination of the relation of Bishop Seabury to the Protestant Episcopal Church, we do not desire to detract from his estimable traits of character, his earnestness of purpose, or his mental endowments. These we fully acknowledge, as we do those of his worthy Revolutionary contemporary, Archbishop Carroll, a divine equally esteemed. At the same time, we are bound in the interests of historical truth, and of sound religion, to show how the false opinions and reactionary measures of this able, Non-Juring clergyman, were substituted in the Protestant Episcopal Prayer Book for the antagonistic, Protestant, and Scriptural principles of the Revolutionary Statesmen and Divines who framed the Constitution and Liturgy of 1785.

BISHOP SEABURY'S ERROR WITH RESPECT TO THE LORD'S SUPPER.

From his sermon on the Holy Eucharist, Vol. I, we quote: "It being admitted that Christ did offer Himself—His natural body and blood—His whole humanity to God, a sacrifice for the sin of the world; and having been shown that He did not offer Himself on the Cross, but was, in everything that related to His Crucifixion, merely passive; it may be asked, when did He offer Himself? I answer, in the Institution of the Holy Eucharist * * *. As He could not wound and kill His own natural body, and shed His own blood, He made this offering in a *mystery*, that is, under the *emblems of bread and wine* * * *. The truth of this position, that Christ, under the emblems or symbols of bread and wine in the Holy Eucharist, *offered* or *gave* His natural body and blood for the sin of the world will further appear, etc. It now having been proved that Christ did, at the Institution of the Eucharist, offer His natural body and blood to God, an expiatory sacrifice for sin, under the symbols and representation of bread broken and wine poured out, and consecrated by blessing and thanksgiving, etc. * * *. It appears, therefore, that the Eucharist is * * * a true and proper sacrifice commemorative of the original sacrifice, and death of Christ for our deliverance from sin and death—a memorial made before God to put Him in mind, etc. * * *. The elements being thus made authoritative representations or symbols of Christ's crucified body and blood, are in a proper capacity to be offered to God as the great and acceptable sacrifice of the Christian Church. Accordingly the oblation, which is the highest, most solemn, and proper act of Christian worship is then immediately made." pp. 150–9.

The doctrine, that the propitiatory sacrifice of our Lord was made on the occasion of the Institution of the Holy Communion, and not on the Cross, is here distinctly and repeatedly asserted.

These words, and many more of like meaning, sufficiently prove that Bishop Seabury's views were in direct antagonism to those of the English Reformers, and plainly contain the germ of Popery.

They prove also, that Bishop Provoost and others were justified in their stern opposition to the influence of such anti-Protestant teaching.

BISHOP SEABURY'S VIEW OF THE EFFECTS OF BAPTISM.

"The power of God's grace has been supposed always to accompany the due celebration of His ordinances. Baptism has ever been regarded, not only as the sign and seal of regeneration, but as the means by which the regenerating influences of the Holy Ghost have been conveyed, and therefore it is called the washing of regeneration * * *. This baptism our Saviour transferred into His Church, and made it the sacrament of initiation into it, and the medium of that new and spiritual birth, without which no one can enter into the kingdom of God, any more than he can enter into this world any other way than by his natural birth * * *. If the blessing of Christ did procure for those infants the grace and Holy Spirit of God, where is the absurdity of believing that baptism by Christ's appointment, and performed by His authorized minister, should procure the grace of regeneration and the Holy Spirit for those infants who come to it by the faith of their parents?" Vol. I. 21. 111, 121.

BISHOP SEABURY'S VIEWS OF THE MINISTRY.

"St. Paul's says: 'We Christians have an altar, whereof they have no right to eat which serve the tabernacle.' Now, where there is an altar, there must be a sacrifice, and a priest to offer it. And as Christ's Apostles were at its institution, authorized by Him to offer the Christian sacrifice of bread and wine, no doubt can remain of their being the priests of the Christian Church in the most proper sense * * *. The administration of the sacraments has been proved to belong exclusively to the ministers of Christ in virtue of His commission to them. They are therefore dispensers of those gifts and graces of the Holy Spirit which accompany those ordinances. The power of administration depending so directly upon the commission of Christ to His Apostles, he who holds no part of it by an uninterrupted succession of ordinations can have no pretense to meddle with them * * *. The Scriptures having pointed out no other way of communicating this authority, but by the hands of the Apostles of the Church —they, I mean, who have succeeded the original Apostles in the power of ordination and government— by them only can this authority be now imparted * * *. Since the Holy Apostles did, in obedience to Christ, and under the direction of the Holy Ghost, transmit to others the powers they received from Him, constituting bishops, presbyters and deacons, as three orders of ministers in His Church; it is the duty of all Christians to submit to that government which they, the Apostles, have instituted, and not to run after the new-fangled scheme of parochial episcopacy, of which the Bible knows nothing, and of which the Christian Church knew nothing till a little more than two centuries ago." Sermons I. 21, 62, 88.

Sufficient has been quoted to show how widely Bishop Seabury differed in his view of the Lord's Supper, Baptism, and the Ministry from the teachings of the Prayer Book of 1785, and why Bishop Provoost, Jay, and other earnest Protestants, depreciated the baleful influence of such doctrines upon their infant Communion.

The doctrines of this eccentric divine with respect to *the Church* are correspondingly narrow, unreasonable, and unscriptural.

A FURTHER OBJECTION.

Moreover, the extremely offensive language of Bishop Seabury, with respect to Christians of other folds, created a natural and intense opposition to him. With respect to the Methodists, he writes to Dr. Smith, "the plea of the Methodists is something like impudence. Mr. Wesley is only a presbyter, and all his ordinations Presbyterian, and in direct opposition to the Church of England. And they can have no pretense for calling themselves Churchmen till they return to the Unity of the Church, which they have unreasonably, unnecessarily, and wickedly broken, by their separation and schism." Bishop White's Mem. p. 287.

SEABURY ON CALVINISTS.

Calvin and the Presbyterians were especially obnoxious to him. He writes: "Calvin was undoubtedly a man of abilities, and his whole conduct shows that he was a man of an assuming, intrepid, and vindictive temper. He busied himself in everything which concerned the Reformation, and with everybody who had any influence in it. At last he fixed himself at the head of the Protestants and became their Pope. Little was done, little was taught but as Calvin liked and advised * * *. Talk with a Calvinist on religion, and begin where you will, you will soon get into election and reprobation and irresistible grace. You would think religion consisted of nothing else * * *. Predestination is to the mind what the jaundice is to the body. The whole Bible appears tinctured with a sickly, yellow hue, when the predestinarian looks into it, especially if he be of a morose and vindictive temper, as most commonly is the case." Sermons, vol. II. 234–98.

SEABURY ON WHITFIELD.

When the apostolic Whitfield, who crossed the ocean to this Continent seven times to preach the Gospel, came to his vicinity, Dr. Seabury was greatly troubled. He writes: "We have had a long visit from Mr. Whitfield in this Colony where he has preached frequently, especially in the city of New York, and in this island, and I am sorry to say he has had more influence than formerly, and I fear has done a great deal of mischief. His tenets and methods of preaching have been adopted by many of the dissenting teachers, and this town (Jamaica) in particular has a continual, I had almost said a daily, succession of strolling preachers and exhorters." Again he writes:

"Without Bishops the Church can not flourish in America, and unless the Church be well supported and prevail, this whole Continent will be overrun with infidelity and deism, Methodism and New Light, with every species of skepticism and enthusiasm, and without a Bishop on the spot I fear it will be impossible to keep the Church herself pure and undefiled." Doc. Hist. N. Y., IV. 327–30.

The ten Tory clergymen who secretly sent Dr. Seabury across the water for consecration, appear to have been as strongly impressed with the impending danger to religion, for they appeal for Seabury's consecration on this ground: "that the Church of God might not become extinct here." On this language, the *International Review* for July, 1881, p. 327 in an article on Bishop Seabury, remarks: "The vitality and all the effective benedictive agency of the Christian religion on character, conduct and human life, and the institutions of a Continent, are made dependent upon a subtile and unique virtue running through an unbroken line of men, like electricity on a continuous wire, conveying authority from one to another by a touch."

This is a strikingly correct definition of the Apostolic Succession chimera, so widely prevalent in the Protestant Episcopal Communion.

BISHOP SEABURY ON THE POSITION OF THE LAITY.

But there was no view of Bishop Seabury more repellant to the men who had fought through the Revolution, and framed the Prayer Book of 1785 on the principles of William III and his noble Bishops, than that respecting the position of the laity in the Church. It was truly, in the language of Bishop Provoost, an "absurd and slavish tenet."

He starts with the theory that laymen have no Scriptural right to partake of the Holy Communion. He seems not to have been familiar with St. Paul's first letters to the Corinthians, where not only is the right of the laity to this ordinance established, but inasmuch as that Church appears to have had no pastor at that period, the right of a layman to administer the rite in an emergency, can be reasonably inferred. Bishop Seabury says, vol. I, p. 146: "No Church that I know of excludes the laity from the Communion; though (the practice of the primitive Church excepted,) they have no direct authority for their admission. All that can be alleged from Scripture, in favor of lay communion, may be explained away in the same manner in which the Presbyterians explain away Episcopal government, &c."

NO AUTHORITY FROM THE PEOPLE.

On p. 40, he remarks: "With respect to the government of the Church, I must as a faithful minister of Christ, and a governor in His Church, bear my testimony against the position that *ecclesiastical or spiritual powers are in any sense derived from the people, or from any human authority.*"

The Bishop appears to have forgotten that several of the most noted Bishops of antiquity were appointed by the people, without the co-operation of the clergy, and in some cases, apparently without receiving consecration. Chrysostom, Ambrose, Martin, Eustatius, Eraclius and Miletus, are noted instances. See Colman, Christ. Antiq. p. 67.

Among other extravagant opinions of this prelate was that the appointment of pastors be confirmed by the Bishop; that it was his prerogative to prepare the Liturgy for his Diocese; that when our Saviour used the expression, "Hear the Church," he had reference to the *governors of the Church*—See pp. 47, 75. Indeed, the word "Church" seemed to be in Seabury's mind almost identical with "the clergy."

LAYMEN UNAUTHORIZED TO LEGISLATE.

It is not wonderful that he was totally opposed to the admission of the laity to Convention, with the privilege of legislating, and much less to their possession of co-ordinate power. On this point he was in direct antagonism to the Revolutionary statesmen. Yet Seabury, by the weak compliance of Bishop White, Dr. Smith, and others, obtained a complete triumph over all opposition. Dr. Hawks in his comment on Article III, Const. P. E. Church, says: "In the General Convention of September, 1789, Bishop Seabury with the churches under his care came into the union, but not until a change had been made in this Article. They made it a condition that this article should be so modified 'as to declare explicitly the rights of the Bishops when sitting in a separate house to originate and propose acts for the concurrence of the other house of Convention; and to negative such acts proposed by the other house as they may disapprove.' This modification was agreed to, and thus to Bishop Seabury belongs the merit of having made the Bishops an equal and co-ordinate power in the work of our general and ecclesiastical legislation."

THE PREDOMINATING INFLUENCE OF THE CLERGY CONFIRMED.

Thus, instead of giving a co-ordinate power to the laity as representing the great body of the Church, the legislative power of the clergy was more than duplicated. A vote by orders was allowed the clergy in the lower house at all times, and if the clergy were defeated, the question must then run the gauntlet of the House of Bishops, and by a simple majority in that body of overpowering influence, the unanimous voice of the laity, together with that of the clergy, might be smothered, the House of Bishops at the same time *sitting with closed doors.* In this disastrous and indefensible erection of a legislative body analogous to the English House of Lords, but with greater legislative privilege and power, having a mysterious, undefined, exclusive prerogative, and having a life tenure, none of the great Revolutionary statesmen had a hand. The work of Jay and Duane; Peters and Shippen; Page and Pinckney; Brearley and Griffin; grand Christian statesmen and heroes, was overthrown by men of smaller make. It has required the disastrous experience of near a century to undo the work of Seabury, and to enable Bishop Cummins to re-erect the Church of the Revolution, of the Reformation, of the Apostles, on its ancient foundations of Scriptural Truth, and Ecclesiastical Freedom.

MINOR ECCENTRICITIES OF BISHOP SEABURY.

We have but space to enumerate among the further eccentricities of this prelate, his claim, as the prerogative of a Bishop, to confer the degree of D. D.: his occasional practice of wearing a mitre as a badge of office, and of signing his name as Samuel, Connecticut, &c., in imitation of the feudal custom of the English prelates of the House of Lords. His expressed preference for the first and half reformed Book of Edward

VI, to the later Revision of 1552, of the Reformers; in which he has now many Protestant Episcopal imitators; coupled with other mediæval Non-Juring sentiments, created a wide and just suspicion as to his want of sympathy with the established Evangelical doctrines of the English Reformation. Sermons I, p. 58; II, 47.

THE OPPONENTS OF BISHOP SEABURY FULLY VINDICATED.

As men faithful to the truth of Scripture, to the Reformed Religion, and to Religious and Civil Freedom, Bishop Provoost and John Jay, with other enlightened and liberty-loving Episcopalians, were compelled to earnestly oppose his connection with their Church, as one of its Bishops. They felt assured that his eccentricities and extravagances of doctrine, in addition to other valid objections, would be pernicious and destructive to the infant Church, in leading minds into erroneous and unsafe views, and in raising obstacles to its growth of an insuperable character. The present state of the Protestant Episcopal Church with respect to sympathy with mediæval doctrine and its allowance of Semi-Romish rites; the predominating influence and authority of the name and opinions of Bishop Seabury, the centennial of whose consecration is now being commemorated with much *eclat* throughout that Communion; furnishes an ample vindication of their wisdom, and faithfulness to the Truth, to the mind of every unprejudiced, independent, patriotic, American Christian.

"Distance may lend enchantment to the view." We trust, however, that these *facts and authorities*, which in the interest of Truth we have here presented, may serve to open the eyes, and clear the vision of some who are dazzled by the glare of this *Ignis Fatuus* of an imaginary, mysterious, undefined, exclusive Divine right, in a fancied third order of Bishops in the Christian Ministry; may free some souls from their unconscious subjection to the Traditions and Commandments of men, and may lead them into the enjoyment of the whole Truth.

POLITICAL OBJECTIONS TO BISHOP SEABURY.

In addition to the objections made to Bishop Seabury on account of his unsound and extravagant doctrines and eccentric ideas, there was a hostile feeling extensively felt towards him on account of his active partisanship during the Revolutionary War, in opposition to the measures of Congress. There were English rectors and missionaries who held to the doctrine of passive obedience, who yet quietly and devotedly fulfilled the duties of their calling during this stormy period, and were greatly respected. Such were Dr. Bass, in Massachusetts, and Dr. Beach in New Jersey. In Connecticut, New York, and New Jersey there was scarcely an Episcopal clergyman, and comparatively few laymen, of that Communion, who sided with the Colonists. This is evident from the letter of Dr. Charles Inglis, Rector of Trinity Church, New York, on the State of the Church, written October, 1776.

He says: "I have the pleasure to assure you that *all* the Society's Missionaries, without excepting one, in New Jersey, New York, Connecticut, and as far as I can learn, in the other New England Colonies, have proved themselves faithful, loyal subjects in these trying times; and have to the utmost of their power opposed the spirit of disaffection and rebellion, which has involved this Continent in the greatest calamities. I must add that all the other clergy of our Church in the above Colonies, though not in the Society's service, have observed the same line of conduct."

THE PRESBYTERIAN CLERGY SUSTAIN CONGRESS.

On the other hand he says of " the Presbyterian ministers:" " I do not know one of them, nor have I been able, after strict inquiry, to hear of any who did not by preaching and every effort in their power, promote all the measures of Congress, however extravagant." " The present rebellion is certainly one of the most causeless, unprovoked and unnatural that ever disgraced any country; a rebellion marked with peculiarly aggravated circumstances of guilt and ingratitude * * * very few of the laity (members of our Church) who were respectable, or men of property, have joined the rebellion." The general state of the Episcopal mind is evident from this document, and the part taken at the North, by that Denomination with respect to the Revolution. See Doc. His. N. York, IV. 1049-66.

Dr. Inglis states that the clergy not being allowed to pray for the King, refused to hold public service, and shut up their churches. This was universal in Connecticut, New Jersey and New York, except when protected by English bayonets; and in Pennsylvania, except in Philadelphia, and in one or two missions. All who wished to worship God in public were consequently compelled to attend the Non-Episcopal Churches.

When the American Army entered New York, Dr. Inglis writes: "I shut up the churches."

After the disastrous Battle of Long Island, when New York was abandoned, and the Dutch Reformed Churches filled by the Tories with American prisoners, who were treated with savage barbarity, Dr. Inglis writes: "I opened one of the churches, and solemnized Divine Service, when all the inhabitants gladly attended, and joy was lighted up in every countenance on the restoration of our public worship; for very few remained but such as were members of our Church."

SEABURY A GUIDE TO GENERAL CLINTON.

Dr. Seabury was now in New York acting as Chaplain to the British forces. He preached a sermon to stimulate the army against the rebels, which was printed by the Governor, and widely scattered in both countries. In April, 1775, with others, he had signed a protest in which he declared his "honest abhorrence of all unlawful Congresses and Committees," and determination "at the hazard of our lives and properties to support the King and Constitution."

In Hamilton's Life by his son, there is presented another reason for the popular odium against Dr. Seabury. It was the authorship of Tracts marked by great ability and asperity against the popular cause.

"In a neighboring Colony the exasperation rose so high, that at a meeting of the County, the pamphlets were tarred and feathered, and nailed to the pillory amid the shouts of the people. * * * The efforts to introduce episcopacy into America were recurred to, and the abject devotion displayed by some of the clerical dependents of the Crown, and their unguarded avowal of their sentiments, increased the odium." It was proposed by some "that author and publisher should be indicted for treasonable designs." Vol. I. p.

28. The Tracts were the joint productions of Dr. Seabury and Rev. Isaac Wilkins.

But what made Seabury the most obnoxious of all the Episcopal clergy was the active part he took in assisting General Clinton in his Campaigns. In the Doc. Hist. New York, IV. p. 1063, we read: " Mr. Seabury considered it his most prudent course to close his church, 'as there could be neither prayers nor sermon till he could pray for the King.' On the retreat of the American Army, after the Battle of Long Island, Mr. S. withdrew within the British lines, where (Hawkins says) he was very useful to General Clinton, whom he furnished with plans and maps of the roads and rivers in the county of Westchester, which could not but be highly serviceable."

The same statement may be found in Reed's life of General Reed, II, 170. "The established Church and its clergy were, it may be concluded, no favorites in this part of the United States. They were objects of ill-concealed enmity, which neither the unquestioned patriotism of a portion of the laity, nor Dr. White's republicanism could disarm. Nor was it unnatural, for the conduct of the clergy in New York and New Jersey had been most offensive. Mr. Seabury by his own showing was a guide to Sir Henry Clinton in 1776, and Odell, a refugee from New York, was a regular contributor of clever ribaldry to *Kingston's Royal Gazette*. He (Odell) appears to have been a medium of communication between Gustavus (Arnold) and John Anderson (Andre) in 1780."

SEABURY THE SUBJECT OF POLITICAL SATIRE.

We have further evidence of the feeling with which Seabury and other Tory rectors were regarded, in "Trumbull's McFingal," a patriotic satire largely directed against the Episcopal clergy.

> "Have not our Cooper and our Seabury
> Sung hymns like Barak and old Deborah,
> Proved all intrigues to set you free,
> Rebellion 'gainst the powers that be;
> Brought over many a Scripture text,
> That used to wink at rebel sects,
> Coaxed wayward ones to favor regents,
> And paraphrased them to obedience."

RESULTS JUSTIFY THE OPPOSITION OF BISHOP PROVOOST.

The active and persistent partisanship of Bishop Seabury in behalf of King and Parliament, and the "enmity" felt towards him especially, for his notorious antagonism to Congress, certainly justifies the determined efforts which Provoost, Jay and Duane made to save the infant Church from connection with this offensive Loyalist. They foresaw the disastrous effects which would necessarily result from the predominating influence of this energetic divine, now advanced to the Episcopate. They knew full well that at the South, where their Church was the strongest in numbers, and intensely patriotic, such a union would be generally and indignantly resisted. The sad result followed.

Though at the first Convention, after the Seabury accession, there were eighty clergymen in Virginia and the Carolinas, there were but seventy-seven in New England, New York, New Jersey and Pennsylvania combined. In twenty years from this time, there was not one Protestant Episcopal candidate for orders, the Church at large was in a confessed decline, while at the South it was little more than a name. Such were the natural results of the failure of the wise and patriotic efforts of Provoost, Jay, Duane, and others to preserve the Constitution and Prayer Book of 1785; such the legitimate and disastrous consequences of the triumph of Seabury and his friends.

THE CIRCUMSTANCES OF BISHOP SEABURY'S ELECTION OBJECTIONABLE.

Ten ministers, stipendiaries of an English Society, who had shut their churches up during the war, and thus deprived the people of all opportunity of Liturgical worship in the use of the Episcopal Service, met in Woodbury, March 1783, and requested Dr. Seabury to go to England, and be consecrated a Bishop, for a land with which they had no civil connection, for we do not learn that they had taken a new oath of allegiance; they were still British subjects. Beardsley in Hist. of Ch. of Connecticut, Vol. I. p. 346, says: "They went into no formal election of a Bishop as takes place in these days."

A DEED DONE IN A CORNER.

Moreover, the deed was done with the utmost secrecy. It "was kept a profound secret even from their most intimate friends of the laity." p. 347. None of the twenty thousand laymen of Connecticut knew that these ten clergymen, who had been neglecting their spiritual interests for seven years by depriving them of Public Service, had officiously and unwarrantedly undertaken to select a spiritual governor to rule over them. The motive that prompted this presumptuous act was " that the Church of God might not have become extinct here." If the ministers of the Congregational Church had closed their churches, as these had done, this danger might certainly have existed. The clergy not being allowed to pray publicly for an earthly King, the people were not by them permitted to pray publicly to the King of Kings.

The *International Review*, July, 1881, p. 319, states: " The approval of some clergymen in New York, and of Carlton, the British Governor and General, still there, was procured under the same secrecy." This whole act of these Connecticut clergy in surreptitiously procuring a Bishop for America, singularly enough, was British and Tory throughout. It had not, however, the stamp of British honesty. Strangly enough, as the same *Review* states : " Only about a year afterward, in May, 1774, at a meeting of Episcopal clergy and laymen from New York, Pennsylvania, and New Jersey, held at New Brunswick, did the secret of the Connecticut movement come to the knowledge of their brethren." Nor is it strange that Dr. Smith, one of these clergymen, wrote to the Scottish Bishops, that Dr. Seabury was chosen "at the instigation of a few clergymen that remain * * *. See, if you value you own peace and advantage as a Christian Society, that your Bishops meddle not with this consecration." If the Scottish Bishops had heeded this advice, the Church in America might have been preserved from an irremediable disaster. See Hawks' & Perry's Reprint of Journal Gen. Conventions.

Seabury was utterly unsuccessful in his application to the English Bishops for consecration. The *International Review*, p. 321, states that: "Finding the Prelates so divided in opinion about his request, Seabury was forced to continue the secrecy of his scheme in England, lest the dissenters might be tempted to ask our authorities in America to oppose it."

Secrecy was stamped upon the undertaking from its first contrivance, to its final success. It hardly has a parallel in history. "He that doeth Truth cometh to the light, that his deeds may be made manifest that they are wrought in God."

THE VALIDITY OF SEABURY'S ELECTION DOUBTFUL.

The validity of Seabury's appointment to the Episcopate may be very justly questioned. There was no election by the people such as was required in the Primitive Church. Mosheim, a standard historian, states: "To them (the multitude or people) belonged the appointment of the bishops or presbyters, as well as of the inferior ministers * * *. Nothing whatever, of any moment, could be determined or carried into effect without their knowledge or concurrence." De Rebus Cristianor., Bk. 1, § 45. But Seabury was elected without the knowledge or concurrence of an American layman, and by a few clergymen who were not citizens of the country for which he was designated. His election being thus unauthorized, and vitiated *ab initio*, could any succeeding consecration remove the *bar sinister?* For consecration is merely a public acknowledgement or confirmation of an office obtained through election. The mind of the Spirit is known in the vote of a praying people. No election of a bishop not fair or honest, can be held to be valid, unless we believe that heaven smiles on craft or cunning. Too many Episcopal elections have been vitiated by intrigue and stratagem.

We are not, therefore, suprised to learn that, "the prelates were sensitive also about making a strolling or mendicant bishop without a sustaining See. A year's patient and earnest effort in London, at his own charges, did not one whit advance Seabury's wishes. When one prelate was to a degree conciliated another would start an objection. Perhaps all of them became a little weary of Seabury's presence and persistency." Inter. Rev. p. 322.

SEABURY'S APPLICATION TO THE SCOTCH CHURCH.

The application to the Scotch Non-Juring Bishops was strikingly appropriate to the circumstances under which Seabury had been sent. "This was a discredited and disfranchised succession from the prelacy of the old Scotch Church, who at the Revolution would not forswear themselves to the Stuart dynasty by swearing allegiance to their royal substitutes. There were at the time of Seabury's errand four bishops of this sort, with forty-two clergy under them. They were under the ban, and in ill odor in England, and disesteemed by their brother prelates. By an Act of George II., a penalty of six months' imprisonment with final transportation was denounced upon any members of the Communion, more than five, who should meet for worship, and this could only be in a private dwelling. They were forbidden to officiate at all in England." Inter. Rev. p. 322.

Here certainly was a remarkably appropriate resort for one thus clandestinely elected. Seabury had found at last suitable consecrators. He was consecrated on condition, that the Connecticut Clergy "when in Scotland should not hold Communion in sacred offices with those persons, who, under pretense of ordination by an English or Irish bishop, do or shall take upon themselves to officiate in any part of the National Church of Scotland, and whom the Scottish bishops cannot help looking upon as schismatical intruders, etc." This condition could not have displeased Seabury, as he looked upon all Non-Episcopal clergymen as schismatical intruders into the sacred office, and this is also the avowed opinion of his American disciples. The line of secrecy was also carried out with respect to the consecration sermon, which was published without the name of the preacher, or of the place where the act was performed.

HIS CONSECRATION NOT RECOGNIZED IN ENGLAND.

We are not surprised to learn "His consecration was not recognized in London. He was not addressed by his title of bishop, nor invited by any of the clergy to preach. To a letter to the secretary of the Society of which he had been for thirty-one years a devoted missionary, asking about the continuance of his salary, he received a letter addressed to the 'Rev. Dr. Seabury,' that he was no longer one of its missionaries, its rule comprehending only British dependencies." Inter. Rev.

p. 323. Are Bishop Provoost and his friends to be condemned for extending similar treatment to this divine ?

We have enumerated these plain facts with respect to Bishop Seabury; his doctrines, his position and acts during the American Revolution; the manner of his election and consecration; (and we have furnished the proofs of all our statements), in order to vindicate and justify the action of those who earnestly opposed all ecclesiastical connection with him; who refused to recognize the validity of his election and consecration to the Episcopate; and who, on this account, have been widely vilified and abused by the admirers and followers of this now much magnified prelate.

WHY THE FACTS HERE NARRATED ARE NOT GENERALLY KNOWN.

The circumstances connected with the early history of the Protestant Episcopal Church in this country are not widely known, for the reason that the documents are not easy of access. Few have written concerning these important transactions. Bishop White, who was well qualified to describe them, has furnished but scant materials. His own reputation for wisdom and consistency would not be advanced by a minute narration of the early history of the Protestant Episcopal Church. The best work of Bishop White was the Constitution and Prayer Book of 1785 and 86; his clearest and ablest production was his Tract in 1782, urging the organization of the Church on a Provisional basis; the noblest body of men with whom he co-operated, were the grand Revolutionary Statesmen and Soldiers of those Primary Conventions. On this pre-eminent period of his life, he has not seen fit to dwell. Through want of wisdom and consistency, through a marvelous weakness of judgment and foresight at this critical juncture, he allowed a departure from the sound, Protestant, Republican principles of the Primary Conventions.

There has never been exhibited in all history a more remarkable ecclesiastical somerset than the substitution of the Seabury Constitution and Prayer Book, for that of Jay and Duane, Peters, Page, and Pinckney. To this Prayer Book and Constitution, Bishop White and Dr. William Smith had given their hearty, public concurrence. They had been foremost in their construction. The Preface to the Prayer Book, prepared by Dr.

Smith and thoroughly endorsed by Bishop White, had plainly and fully stated that the Protestant Episcopal Church had based its Reforms and Reunion on the plan and principles of William III. and his bishops, as set forth in the *Review* of 1689. Bishop White writes to Dr. Smith, February 10, 1786: "I express my approbation of your Preface * * *. I like it both in plan and execution." Dr. Smith writes to Bishop White, April 9, 1786: "In the Scot's and Edward VIth Liturgy, the prayer was exceptionable, and leaning much to transubstantiation." See Hawks' and Perry's Reprint of Journal. Yet these clergy now surrendered to Bishop Seabury, who represented the party of James II., and while they carefully rejected this prayer from the Book of 1785, they allowed it entrance in the Book of 1789, where it has remained with other erroneous doctrines thus incorporated, to deface and corrupt the Church; to produce sorrow, contention, and alienation, and finally ecclesiastical separation, among brethren of the same fold.

Seabury and the New England Clergy notoriously represented the Non-Juring party of James II.; White, Provoost and Griffith, the Reforming Bishops of William III. The doctrines of the latter are in the Book of 1785 and in that of 1874; the doctrines of the former in that of 1789, the present Protestant Episcopal Book. These two antagonistic principles are again in conflict.

NON-JURORS, BARRIERS TO REFORM AND FREEDOM IN ENGLAND AND AMERICA.

And like as the salutary reforms of the Bishops of William III. were rendered nugatory largely on account of the dread entertained of the successful machinations of the Non-Jurors, in case the English Liturgy had been changed; so in like manner were White and Smith largely influenced in their surrender to Seabury by the threat that if he was not received on his own terms, Jarvis, of Connecticut, already selected, with Parker, of Boston, would be sent to Scotland for Consecration. Thus another and similar schism would result by the action of the American Non-Jurors. The fear of such consequences triumphed over the demands of consistency of doctrine and action, of adhesion to their principles, enunciated distinctly in the Constitution and Prayer Book of 1785, and by Bishop White most forcibly in his carefully prepared Tract on a Provisional Episcopacy, published December, 1782.

THE PREFACE OF 1789 ENDORSES THAT OF 1785.

The most marvelously inconsistent feature of this strange transaction, perhaps, is the declaration in the Preface of the Book of 1789, written by Bishop White, as follows: "A commission for a Review was issued in the year 1689, but this great and good work miscarried at that time." Thus, notwithstanding this good Bishop had publicly revised the Book of 1785, on the plan of that "great and good work," and then abandoned it for the work of its avowed enemies, he and the Protestant Episcopal Church have in the words quoted from their authorized Preface, endorsed the first Book, that of 1785, and consequently the Book of 1874, that of the Reformed Episcopal Church. This memorable display of a want of consistency in doctrine and action, this want of fidelity to Scriptural Truth, this fear of threats of ecclesiastical division, as were displayed in the reactionary and humiliating measures of 1789, produced the evil results which constrained Bishop Cummins to withdraw from the Protestant Episcopal Communion, and to establish the Reformed Episcopal Church on the avowed basis of the doctrines and principles of the loyal Episcopalians of the American Revolution, identical with those of William III.

INHERENT EVILS IN THE HIGH CHURCH SACERDOTAL SYSTEM.

Devotion to uniformity, to the semblance of unity, a hollow union, have ever been the bane of the Protestant Episcopal Church. The evil is inherent in a system of Sacerdotalism, and of exclusive Divine right, with mysterious, undefined prerogatives. The possession of a more than ordinarily level head, and a heart filled with an uncommon degree of humility and love, are required to make an Episcopate a success under the Protestant Episcopal Regimen. Hence the frequent failures even among those who have excelled as Presbyters. And this evil is often aggravated by the party spirit and selfish schemes which accompany Episcopal elections, when men are chosen not for superior moderation, learning and sanctity, but for devotion to particular party measures, and to some powerful ecclesiastical clique. But the Episcopal system of that Communion is not that of Scripture nor of the Primitive Church. Hence its comparative failure, and its loss of spiritual power and influence.

A GRAND OPPORTUNITY NEEDLESSLY LOST.

If the Protestant Episcopal Church had been wisely permitted to remain on the Protestant, Free, Revolutionary basis, as primarily arranged by its grand founders, there was nothing to prevent its becoming; with a thoroughly purified Liturgy, and a reduced and safely modified Episcopacy, and such a band of pre-eminent laymen, Christian statesmen and heroes; Washington and Jay, Duane and Rutherford, the Morris's and the Livingstons; Duer, Willett and King, Peters and Shippen, the Lees, the Nicholases, the Nelsons, the Marshalls and the Randolphs; Page and Griffin, Pinckney and Rutledge; with clergymen like Provoost and White, William and Robert Smith, Wharton and Pettigrew, Griffith and Madison; the foremost ecclesiastical power in the land. It lost its opportunity, and with that opportunity its crown. This the Methodist Communion has taken, by the superlative wisdom of its leaders, its devotion to a pure and living Gospel, its Christian energy and patriotism. The poor and despised sect, without prestige, without wealth, without men of Revolutionary renown, but blessed of God for fidelity to truth and principle and country, has become the first in the land. Its older, more powerful, more famous and more arrogant sister has taken the position of seventh among the Churches. Tradition substituted for Scripture, the Letter for the Spirit, has brought this to pass. "Not by power, nor by might, but by My Spirit, saith the Lord."

THE TRIUMPH OF THE TRUTH APPROACHING.

The present Era is propitious for the restoration and advancement of sound, Scriptural, and timely American principles. Centennial celebrations are calling public attention to the startling but slightly known facts pertaining to the history of the Protestant Episcopal Church of that memorable period.

Those who will study with candor and attention the subject handled in these notes, will learn that the Reformed Episcopal Church alone can rightfully and legitimately commemorate the work of these Episcopal Revolutionary Fathers; for this Church alone has inherited their principles, and represents their noble, Scriptural undertaking. While the Constitution and Prayer Book of the Protestant Episcopal Church is in direct and irreconcilable antagonism to the published principles, and to the grand work of those great Christian Statesmen; those of the Reformed Episcopal Church are thoroughly identical, being expressly based on the Reform and Revision of the Conventions of 1785 and 1786; made consistent with Scripture; with the Primitive Church; with the Reforming work of William III.; with the principles of the American Revolution.

We leave this intensely interesting subject in confident assurance, that with the growth of Light and Scriptural Truth among Episcopalians in this free land, there will be an ultimate triumph to the true Protestant Episcopacy, as inherited from our venerated Christian Fathers of the American Revolution.

This has been restored and re-affirmed in the Constitution and Prayer Book of the Reformed Episcopal Church.

The hope of the Martyred Reformers of Edward VI., of the wise and charitable Commissioners of William III.; of our patriotic Episcopal Pioneers; of so many departed defenders of Evangelical Truth; will, under God, be realized in the sure and stable progress of this Primitive, Protestant, Scriptural, American Communion.

O, Almighty God, who hast built thy Church upon the foundation of the Apostles and Prophets, Jesus Christ himself being the head Corner Stone; Grant us so to be joined together in unity of spirit by their doctrine, that we may be made a holy temple acceptable unto thee; through Jesus Christ our Lord. *Amen.*

P. S.—Since the preparation of these notes an article appeared in the *Episcopal Recorder*, from the pen of Rev. Dr. E. D. Neill, the Historian of Minnesota, from which a highly interesting extract connected with our subject is given.

"A few years ago there was published for the first time, a remarkable letter in the *New York Churchman*, written on November 8, 1788, to Abernethy, one of the Bishops of the Scotch Episcopal Church, which is recalled at this time. Seabury writes:

'Bishop White, of Philadelphia, seems disposed to an ecclesiastical union, but will take no action or leading part to bring it about. He will ask nothing, and Bishop Provoost seems so elevated with the honor of an English consecration, that he affects to doubt the validity of mine. This may oblige me to establish the Scotch Succession from the re-organization of Charles the Second to what is called the Revolution. How this is best to be done, you can judge better than I can.'

"How humiliating to see a minister of Jesus Christ laying stress on a tactual and Apostolical Succession which after being set apart as a Bishop, he feels at a loss to prove."

www.ingramcontent.com/pod-product-compliance
Lightning Source LLC
Chambersburg PA
CBHW030408170426
43202CB00010B/1531